ENVIRONMENTAL REMEDIATION TECHNOLOGIES, REGULATIONS AND SAFETY

CHEMICAL RISK ASSESSMENT ACTIVITIES IN THE U.S. WITH OVERVIEWS OF CANADA, AUSTRALIA, AND THE WHO

ENVIRONMENTAL REMEDIATION TECHNOLOGIES, REGULATIONS AND SAFETY

Additional books in this series can be found on Nova's website under the Series tab.

Additional e-books in this series can be found on Nova's website under the e-book tab.

ENVIRONMENTAL REMEDIATION TECHNOLOGIES, REGULATIONS AND SAFETY

CHEMICAL RISK ASSESSMENT ACTIVITIES IN THE U.S. WITH OVERVIEWS OF CANADA, AUSTRALIA, AND THE WHO

NAOMI SUTTON
EDITOR

New York

NOTICE TO THE READER

Library of Congress Cataloging-in-Publication Data

ISBN: 978-1-63485-058-2

Published by Nova Science Publishers, Inc. † New York

CONTENTS

PREFACE

With thousands of chemicals in commercial use in the United States, decision makers rely on toxicity assessment information to examine the risks these substances may pose. Several key federal agencies—including the Agency for Toxic Substances and Disease Registry (ATSDR), the Environmental Protection Agency (EPA), the National Institute for Occupational Safety and Health (NIOSH), the National Toxicology Program (NTP), and the Occupational Safety and Health Administration (OSHA)—as well as state agencies, assess the toxicity of chemicals. This book describes the chemical toxicity assessment activities selected federal and state agencies undertake; assesses the extent to which these federal agencies' chemical toxicity assessment activities are fragmented, overlapping, or duplicative; and assesses the extent to which these federal and state agencies coordinate their chemical toxicity assessment activities and challenges in doing so.

In: Chemical Risk Assessment Activities … ISBN: 978-1-63485-058-2
Editor: Naomi Sutton

Chapter 1

CHEMICAL ASSESSMENTS: AGENCIES COORDINATE ACTIVITIES, BUT ADDITIONAL ACTION COULD ENHANCE EFFORTS*

United States Government Accountability Office

WHY GAO DID THIS STUDY

With thousands of chemicals in commercial use in the United States, decision makers rely on toxicity assessment information to examine the risks these substances may pose. Several key federal agencies— including ATSDR, EPA, NIOSH, NTP, and OSHA—as well as state agencies, assess the toxicity of chemicals.

GAO was asked to review chemical toxicity assessment activities. This report (1) describes the chemical toxicity assessment activities selected federal and state agencies undertake; (2) assesses the extent to which these federal agencies' chemical toxicity assessment activities are fragmented, overlapping, or duplicative; and (3) assesses the extent to which these federal and state agencies coordinate their chemical toxicity assessment activities and challenges in doing so. GAO selected five key federal agencies that assess chemicals, and a nonprobability sample of agencies in 10 states that provide a

* This is an edited, reformatted and augmented version of a United States Government Accountability Office publication, No. GAO-14-763, dated September 2014.

range of assessment activities. GAO reviewed federal agency documentation and compiled summaries of chemical toxicity assessment activities and compared them with one another. GAO interviewed officials from these agencies, representatives from industry, and other stakeholders.

What GAO Recommends

GAO recommends that the Director of OSTP encourage the NSTC to support relevant federal agency officials' efforts to address, as appropriate, the agencies' cross-cutting coordination challenges. OSTP did not provide official written comments, but instead provided technical comments, which GAO incorporated as appropriate.

What GAO Found

The federal agencies GAO reviewed—the Agency for Toxic Substances and Disease Registry (ATSDR), the Environmental Protection Agency (EPA), the National Institute for Occupational Safety and Health (NIOSH), the National Toxicology Program (NTP), and the Occupational Safety and Health Administration (OSHA)—undertake distinct chemical toxicity assessment activities that differ in type and purpose and are driven in part by statutory requirements; the 10 states GAO reviewed largely rely on federal agencies' assessment activities. For example, ATSDR's toxicity assessment activities include evaluating hazards at contaminated sites and NIOSH's activities include identifying potential health risks to workers. Agency officials from all 10 of the selected states told GAO that they have used assessment information produced by these federal agencies in the last 5 years. Officials from 6 of the 10 states told GAO they rely on federal assessments, and the remaining 4 said that they may produce their own assessments in some cases—for example, when a chemical is of interest to the state but is not a national priority.

The chemical toxicity assessment activities at these five federal agencies are fragmented and overlapping, but GAO did not find evidence that these activities are duplicative. Their activities are fragmented because they address the same broad area of national need—providing information on the toxicity of chemicals. The five agencies' activities overlap because some of them have similar goals— such as identifying the extent to which a chemical may cause cancer—or some target similar beneficiaries—such as the general public. GAO did not find evidence of duplication, however, because the agencies did not engage in the same activities or provide the same services to the same beneficiaries. For example, although both NIOSH and EPA develop chemical toxicity assessment information, NIOSH assesses the potential risks that chemicals pose to working-aged adults in occupational settings, such as over the course of a 40-hour workweek, and EPA assesses risks that chemicals pose to a broader population, including children, typically over the course of an entire lifetime.

Officials from all five federal agencies and 3 of the 10 states told GAO that they have coordinated their chemical toxicity assessment activities and also identified challenges. For example, some agency officials identified constraints on sharing confidential business information because of legal restrictions on dissemination of such information across agencies. The Office of Science and Technology Policy's (OSTP) National Science and Technology Council (NSTC) coordinates science and technology policies across the federal government. All executive department and agencies, whether or not they are represented on the NTSC, are to coordinate science and technology policy through it. Given that NSTC has previously facilitated federal coordination on cross-cutting topics, such as nanotechnology and pharmaceuticals in the environment, and given its purpose, an official from OSTP stated that NSTC could serve an interagency coordinating function to address certain cross-cutting challenges. By having an interagency body to address these, and any future cross-cutting challenges, the five selected federal agencies would be positioned to better coordinate their assessment activities in the most effective and efficient manner.

ABBREVIATIONS

ATSDR	Agency for Toxic Substances and Disease Registry
BMC	Benchmark Concentration
BMCL	Benchmark Concentration Confidence Limit
Ca	potential occupational carcinogen
CalEPA	California Environmental Protection Agency
CBI	confidential business information
CERCLA	Comprehensive Environmental Response, Compensation, and Liability Act
EPA	Environmental Protection Agency

FSTRAC	Federal-State Toxicology Risk Analysis Committee
IRIS	Integrated Risk Information System
ITRC	Interstate Technology & Regulatory Council
LOAEL	lowest-observed-adverse-effect level
MOU	memorandum of understanding
MRL	Minimal Risk Level
NCEA	National Center for Environmental Assessment
NIOSH	National Institute for Occupational Safety and Health
NOAEL	no-observed-adverse-effect level
NPL	National Priorities List
NSTC	National Science and Technology Council
NTP	National Toxicology Program
OEHHA	Office of Environmental Health Hazard Assessment
OHAT	Office of Health Assessment and Translation
OSHA	Occupational Safety and Health Administration
OSTP	Office of Science and Technology Policy
PEL	permissible exposure limit
ppm	parts per million
PPRTV	Provisional Peer Reviewed Toxicity Value
REL	recommended exposure limit
RfC	inhalation reference concentration
RoC	Report on Carcinogens
STEL	short-term exposure limit
TCE	trichloroethylene
Tox21	Toxicology in the 21st Century
TSCA	Toxic Substances Control Act
TWA	time-weighted average
UF	uncertainty factor

* * *

September 29, 2014

The Honorable Paul Broun
Chairman
Subcommittee on Oversight
Committee on Science, Space, and Technology
House of Representatives

Dear Mr. Chairman:

Thousands of chemicals are in commercial use in the United States, and about 1,000 new chemicals are introduced into commerce each year.[1] These chemicals may provide a wide range of benefits to American consumers, but exposure to certain substances, such as lead or asbestos, may have adverse effects on human health or the environment. Since the 1970s, Congress has enacted various laws to assess and manage risks associated with chemical exposure, and several government agencies have been established to assess and control potential hazards.

Risk assessments—the characterization of the potential adverse health effects of human exposures to environmental hazards—are a key public policy tool for evaluating options for protecting public health and the environment. Chemical risk assessments are a type of risk assessment that examine risks such as the potential for a chemical to cause cancer or the level at which a chemical may cause neurological or developmental effects.[2] Chemical risk assessments typically include four components: (1) hazard identification, (2) dose-response assessment, (3) exposure assessment, and (4) risk characterization.[3] The first two steps—a qualitative hazard identification, and a quantitative dose-response assessment—are commonly referred to together as toxicity assessments.[4] Toxicity values are derived from dose-response assessments. Toxicity assessments weigh available evidence regarding the potential for a chemical to cause adverse effects in exposed individuals and to provide, where possible, an estimate of the relationship between the extent of exposure to a chemical and the increased likelihood and severity of adverse effects. Toxicity assessments combined with information from exposure assessments provide the foundation for characterizing risk (see Figure 1).

Chemical toxicity assessments are the focus of this report and, while many federal agencies perform chemical toxicity assessments, this report focuses on five agencies that follow this four-step risk assessment process: (1) the Agency for Toxic Substances and Disease Registry (ATSDR); (2) the Environmental Protection Agency (EPA); (3) the Centers for Disease Control and Prevention's National Institute for Occupational Safety and Health (NIOSH); (4) the National Institutes of Health's National Toxicology Program (NTP), within the Department of Health and Human Services; and (5) the Occupational Safety and Health Administration (OSHA), within the Department of Labor.[5] In addition, some state agencies develop their own toxicity assessment information. Information derived from these assessments are used to make decisions on a wide range of criteria, such as emissions standards for sources of hazardous air pollutants, workplace safety and health standards, and cleanup levels for contaminated sites.

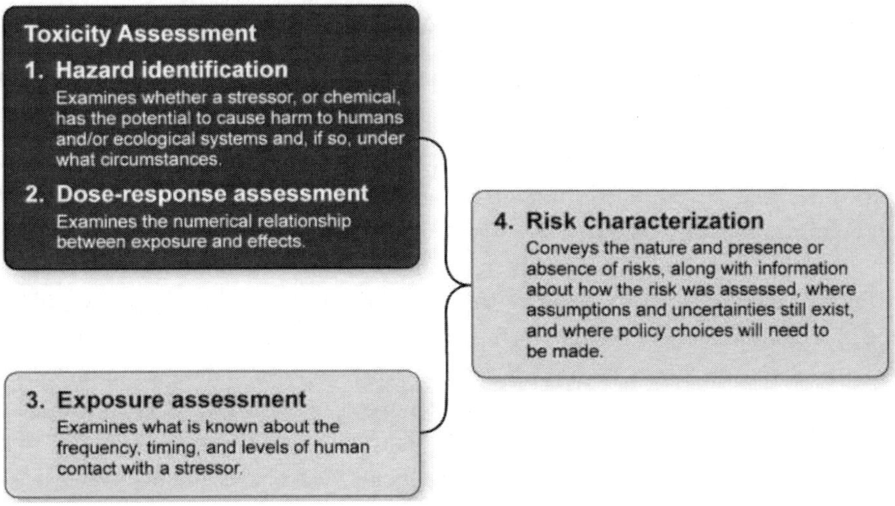

Source: GAO presentation of the risk assessment component of the National Academies' risk assessment and risk management model used by EPA. | GAO-14-763.

Figure 1. The Four Components of the National Academies' Risk Assessment Process.

To assess whether there may be opportunities to save federal resources and help agencies provide more efficient and effective services, GAO often evaluates the potential for fragmentation, overlap, or duplication among federal programs. GAO has defined fragmentation, overlap and duplication as shown in Figure 2.[6]

In 2009, GAO designated the need to transform EPA's process for assessing and controlling toxic chemicals as an area at high risk of waste, fraud, abuse, and mismanagement or in need of broad-based transformation.[7] For example, in March 2008, we reported that data in EPA's Integrated Risk Information System (IRIS)—a human health assessment program that evaluates scientific information on human health effects that may result from exposure to chemicals in the environment—was at serious risk of becoming obsolete because EPA had not been able to keep its existing assessments current or complete assessments of the most important chemicals of concern.[8] In response to our 2008 report and 2009 high-risk designation, EPA revised its IRIS assessment process in May 2009. In December 2011, we reported that these revisions restored EPA's control of the process, increased transparency, and established a 23-month time frame for its less challenging assessments.[9] Progress in other areas, however, has been limited. For example, in our February 2013 update to our high risk list, we found that EPA's initial gains in productivity under the revised process had not been sustained, and that EPA faced both long-standing and new challenges in implementing the IRIS program.[10]

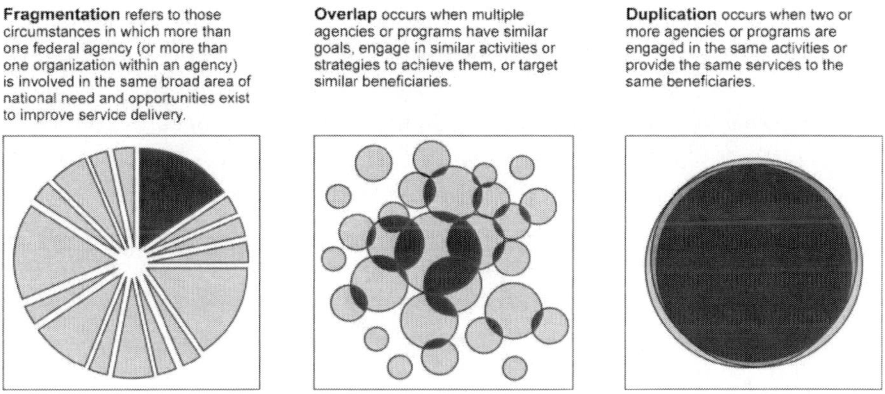

Source: GAO. | GAO-14-763.

Figure 2. GAO's Definitions of Fragmentation, Overlap, and Duplication.

You asked us to provide information on the range of federal chemical toxicity assessment activities. Our objectives for this review are to: (1) describe the chemical toxicity assessment activities selected federal and state agencies undertake; (2) assess the extent to which, if at all, selected federal agencies' chemical toxicity assessment activities are fragmented, overlapping, or duplicative; and (3) assess the extent to which, if at all, selected federal and state agencies coordinate their chemical toxicity assessment activities and the challenges, if any, associated with doing so.

To examine these five federal agencies' chemical toxicity assessment activities, we reviewed publicly available information on these agencies' activities and information from our past reports and compiled summaries of these activities for each agency. We then submitted these summaries to each agency to review for accuracy and incorporated their comments. We also interviewed agency officials as necessary to clarify their comments. We selected a nonprobability sample of 12 state agencies in 10 states that provide a range of chemical assessment activities.[11] We analyzed and reported interview responses using the state as the unit of measure, as opposed to the particular agency. To examine these state agencies' chemical toxicity assessment activities, we conducted structured interviews with officials in these agencies on the scope of their chemical toxicity assessment activities in the last 5 years.

To examine these federal agencies' chemical toxicity assessment activities for fragmentation, overlap, and duplication, we reviewed the summaries of agency toxicity assessment activities and agency documentation that sets forth the scope and purpose of their chemical toxicity assessment activities and compared them with one another and with our definitions of fragmentation, overlap, and duplication. We also further reviewed a nonprobability sample of inhalation toxicity values for 10 selected chemicals as developed by four of the five federal agencies (ATSDR, EPA, NIOSH, and OSHA) and 1 of the 12 selected state agencies, the California Environmental Protection Agency (CalEPA), that conduct toxicity assessment activities for these inhaled chemicals.[12] We selected these 10 chemicals to provide a diverse representation of organic and inorganic chemicals—the two major categories that comprise the universe of all chemicals—with varying structures and chemical properties, which we identified with the assistance of a GAO chemist and a review of chemical toxicity values from federal agencies. We limited our sample to chemicals for which the four of the five selected federal agencies and 1 of the 12 selected state agencies had developed toxicity values. Because this was a nonprobability sample, the information that we obtained on these 10 chemicals is not generalizable to all chemicals.

To examine federal and state agencies' coordination on chemical toxicity assessment activities and any challenges they face, we administered structured interviews to the five selected federal agencies and 12 state agencies. For EPA, which unlike most of the other federal and state agencies has multiple components that conduct chemical toxicity assessments, we also interviewed officials from six program or regional offices to determine the extent to which they coordinate their toxicity assessment activities and identify any challenges to their efforts. In our interviews, we asked officials from each of the five federal agencies whether, and if so, how, their agency had coordinated with each of the other four federal agencies within the past 5 years. The different mechanisms through which agencies coordinate do not necessarily indicate better quality or more effective coordination. Whether the type of coordination mechanism affected quality or effectiveness of interagency coordination is beyond the scope of this review. Agency responses to our structured interviews were further evaluated by considering key practices for collaboration[13] and key considerations for implementing interagency collaborative mechanisms.[14] Appendix I provides additional information on our scope and methodology.

We conducted this performance audit from May 2013 to September 2014 in accordance with generally accepted government auditing standards. Those standards require that we plan and perform the audit to obtain sufficient, appropriate evidence to provide a reasonable basis for our findings and conclusions based on our audit objectives. We believe that the evidence obtained provides a reasonable basis for our findings and conclusions based on our audit objectives.

SELECTED FEDERAL AGENCIES UNDERTAKE DISTINCT CHEMICAL TOXICITY ASSESSMENT ACTIVITIES, AND SELECTED STATES LARGELY RELY ON FEDERAL ASSESSMENTS

The federal agencies we reviewed undertake distinct chemical toxicity assessment activities that differ in type and purpose and are driven largely by agency needs derived from statutory requirements, while officials in the 10 states we reviewed told us that they largely rely on federal agencies' chemical toxicity assessment activities. Officials in the federal agencies we reviewed told us their toxicity assessments activities include evaluating hazards at contaminated sites, identifying potential health risks to workers, and providing information about potential toxic chemicals to regulators. Officials in 6 of the 10 states we reviewed told us they do not conduct their own toxicity assessments and rely instead on existing sources of information primarily supplied by federal agencies, while officials from the remaining 4 states told us they sometimes produce their own assessments but more often rely on federal sources.

Federal Agencies' Chemical Toxicity Assessment Activities Are Driven by Agency Needs Derived from Statutory Requirements and Differ by Type and Purpose

The toxicity assessment activities that these five federal agencies conducted are driven primarily by agency needs derived from the statutory authorities that created the programs. For example, several programs are designed to provide quantitative values that can be used to regulate chemicals, while others provide a qualitative conclusion about the nature of a chemical that can be shared with regulatory agencies and the public. The scope of some assessments is limited to whether the chemical causes cancer, while other assessments look beyond cancer at neurological, respiratory, and reproductive effects (see Figure 3).

ATSDR

ATSDR, a federal public health agency of the U.S. Department of Health and Human Services, prepares toxicity assessments—called toxicological profiles—in response to statutory requirements under the Comprehensive Environmental Response, Compensation, and Liability Act (CERCLA). These profiles provide interpretations of data that can be useful for officials evaluating the chemical hazards at hazardous waste sites.[15] During the development of toxicological profiles, if the agency determines that reliable and sufficient data exist to identify the specific health effects that result from exposure to a hazardous substance, the agency will derive Minimal Risk Levels (MRL). MRLs estimate safe levels of human exposure, are quantitative in nature, and are not based on a consideration of cancer effects. To address cancer, the agency issues separate assessments that include qualitative conclusions regarding cancer effects from human exposure to chemicals.

Although ATSDR is not a regulatory agency, CERCLA requires it to prepare a list, in priority order, of chemicals that are most commonly found at hazardous waste sites on the National Priorities List and which are determined to pose the most significant potential threat to human health.[16] ATSDR then must prepare toxicological profiles on substances on that list. ATSDR's toxicological profiles typically evaluate the effects of exposures to hazardous chemicals for three possible durations: acute (14 days or less), intermediate (15-364 days), and chronic (365 days or more).[17] According to ATSDR, these profiles generally take 18 to 24 months to complete. In recent years, ATSDR has typically completed six or seven toxicological profiles each year; a total of 319 new and updated toxicological profiles have been published or are under development.

Characteristics of toxicity assessment activities:	Selected federal agencies:				
	Agency for Toxic Substances and Disease Registry	Environmental Protection Agency	National Institute for Occupational Safety and Health	National Toxicology Program	Occupational Safety and Health Administration
Purpose of toxicity activities:					
To conduct basic research on workplace chemicals			●		
To evaluate Superfund site health hazards	●	●			
To identify potential health risks to workers		●	●		●
To protect public health and the environment		●			
To provide information about potential toxic chemicals to regulators		●	●	●	
Primary statutory authority(ies):					
Clean Air Act		●			
Clean Water Act		●			
Comprehensive Environmental Response, Compensation, and Liability Act	●	●			
Federal Insecticide, Fungicide, and Rodenticide Act		●			
Mine Safety and Health Act			●		
Occupational Safety and Health Act			●		●
Public Health Service Act				●	
Resource Conservation and Recovery Act		●			
Safe Drinking Water Act		●			
Toxic Substances Control Act		●			

Figure 3. (Continued).

Product types issued by agency(ies):					
Integrated Risk Information System (IRIS)		●			
Minimal Risk Level (MRL) contained in a toxicity profile	●				
Office of Health Assessment and Translation (OHAT) Monograph				●	
Permissible exposure limit (PEL) contained in a toxicity assessment					●
Provisional Peer Reviewed Toxicity Values (PPRTV)		●			
Recommended exposure limit (REL)			●		
Report on Carcinogens (ROC)				●	
Qualitative or quantitative assessment:					
Qualitative	●	●	●	●	●
Quantitative	●	●	●		●

● Agency with characteristic cited

Source: GAO. | GAO-14-763.

Note: Each of the five selected federal agencies address cancer and non-cancer assessments as part of their toxicity assessment activities.

Figure 3. Characteristics of Selected Federal Agencies' Chemical Toxicity Assessment Activities.

ATSDR's MRLs are an estimate of daily human exposure to a hazardous substance at or below which that substance will likely not pose a measurable risk of adverse noncancerous effects—such as neurological, respiratory, and reproductive effects—over a specified time period. MRLs are quantitative in nature, and, according to ATSDR's website, are used as screening values to allow ATSDR health assessors and others to identify contaminants at hazardous waste sites and determine whether further investigation is needed to protect communities from exposure. Although MRLs do not consider possible cancer effects, the agency endorses the use of a narrative statement that conveys the agency's qualitative conclusions regarding cancer effects. In this regard, ATSDR adopts the findings for chemicals addressed by the Department of Health and Human Services' most recent biennial Report on Carcinogens, as coordinated by the National Toxicology Program, to the extent available. These are described in ATSDR's Cancer Policy Framework, which defines what the agency has identified as scientifically credible, internally consistent policy positions to guide ATSDR's activities that address the public health implications of exposure to carcinogens.

EPA

EPA toxicity assessments are generally used to determine the levels of chemical pollutants in the air, land, and water that would not present a significant adverse risk to the public and environment. EPA's ability to effectively implement its mission of protecting public health and the environment is critically dependent on credible and timely assessments of the risks posed by chemicals. Such assessments are the cornerstone of scientifically sound environmental decisions, policies, and regulations under a variety of statutes, such as the Toxic Substances Control Act (TSCA),[18] Safe Drinking Water Act,[19] and the Clean Air Act.[20] EPA activities are also authorized by CERCLA, the Resource Conservation and Recovery Act[21], the Clean Water Act, [22] and the Federal Insecticide, Fungicide, and Rodenticide Act.[23] EPA offices provide a variety of toxicity assessments, including both quantitative and qualitative conclusions about cancer and noncancer effects.

According to EPA officials, three EPA program offices and two EPA regional offices develop a variety of chemical toxicity assessments to assist the agency in fulfilling these statutory requirements.[24] These offices include the following:

- **Office of Research and Development**. The Office of Research and Development produces two types of toxicity assessments,[25] which are developed through its National Center for Environmental Assessment (NCEA). These toxicity assessments provide fundamental information for EPA's risk management decisions, such as whether EPA should establish air emissions standards and water quality standards to protect the public from exposure to particular toxic chemicals. These two types of assessments are as follows:

- NCEA's IRIS is a human health assessment program that evaluates scientific information on human health effects that may result from exposure to chemicals in the environment.[26] These assessments are used by other EPA offices, as well as federal, state, and local environmental agencies, and some international regulatory bodies. IRIS assessments, which currently include information on about 550 chemicals, undergo extensive internal and external peer review and are developed using a process that allows for public input.[27] According to EPA, the importance of the IRIS Program has increased as its program and regional offices have increasingly relied on IRIS toxicity assessments in making environmental protection and risk management decisions.
- NCEA's Provisional Peer Reviewed Toxicity Values (PPRTV) provide information to support cleanup decisions at Superfund sites. NCEA prepares PPRTVs for EPA's Office of Solid Waste and Emergency Response when IRIS toxicity assessments are not available. PPRTVs receive internal review by a panel of NCEA scientists and external peer review by independent scientific experts, but they differ from IRIS values in that they do not undergo as extensive a process of internal and external peer review and public participation as IRIS assessments and are generally completed more quickly.

- **Office of Chemical Safety and Pollution Prevention.** Two offices within the Office of Chemical Safety and Pollution Prevention—the Office of Pollution Prevention and Toxics and the Office of Pesticide Programs—also conduct toxicity assessments as follows:
  - The Office of Pollution Prevention and Toxics is responsible for implementing TSCA, which gives EPA the authority to obtain more information on chemicals and to regulate those chemicals that the agency determines pose unreasonable risks to human health or the environment.[28] The office sometimes uses the hazard and dose response information described in an IRIS toxicity assessment for a particular chemical to develop its own

subsequent toxicity assessments. We reported in March 2013 that officials from the Office of Pollution Prevention and Toxics told us that IRIS assessments are generally used to estimate risks associated with continuous exposures to a pollutant in the air or water rather than the intermittent exposures that workers and consumers are subject to from chemicals contained in products.[29]

- The Office of Pesticide Programs, along with state agriculture offices, registers or licenses pesticides for sale and distribution in the United States under the authority of the Federal Insecticide, Fungicide, and Rodenticide Act. States may also have pesticide licensing programs. Because pesticides must be registered by EPA, the office reviews scientific information on pesticides submitted by pesticide registrants and comprehensive laboratory-based data on multiple routes of exposure. The office uses this information to conduct comprehensive risk assessments for pesticide active ingredients, among other things.

- **Office of Water.** EPA's Office of Water develops a limited number of toxicity assessments to implement the Clean Water Act and Safe Drinking Water Act. According to Office of Water officials, because the IRIS Program can only select and develop a limited number of IRIS assessments at one time, the Office of Water develops its own assessments for chemicals that have less controversy surrounding them and take less time and staff to complete in order to address some of its programmatic needs.
- **Regional offices.** EPA regional offices, which are responsible for the execution of EPA programs within their respective states and territories; EPA officials told us that two EPA regional offices develop chemical toxicity assessments in support of their work. For example, officials in EPA's Region 2 told us that they rely primarily on IRIS toxicity values. They will also use PPRTVs, values from other federal agencies such as ATSDR, and state toxicity values where available.[30] When officials needed toxicity information for a chemical for which none was available, regional officials worked with others at EPA, NTP, and with officials from a potential responsible party to gather toxicity information that led to the development of a PPRTV for that chemical. Similarly, officials in Region 9 told us that they conducted toxicity assessment activities with ATSDR and NCEA that helped identify a previously unknown effect of a chemical commonly found in waterways throughout the country.[31]

NTP

NTP is an interagency program established in 1978 to coordinate chemical toxicity assessment activities across the Department of Health and Human Services. NTP officials told us the program was created to coordinate toxicity testing, strengthen the science base in toxicology, develop and validate improved testing methods, and to provide information about potentially toxic chemicals to health-related regulatory and research agencies, scientific and medical communities, and the public. NTP toxicity assessment activities include these four activities. Under the authority of the Public Health Service Act,[32] the NTP is required to produce the biennial Report on Carcinogens (RoC). Although the NTP's primary effort is to conduct toxicological testing on chemicals, it also performs toxicity assessments drawing on both peer reviewed NTP research and testing information and published literature to produce reports, such as its Office of Health Assessment and Translation (OHAT) monographs.[33] In addition, NTP, in coordination with EPA, the Food and Drug Administration, and the National Institutes of Health, is active in the development of the Toxicology in the 21st Century (Tox21) program, which generates data that are to be provided to risk assessors to use when making decisions about protecting human health and environment. These activities include qualitative conclusions about chemical hazards as follows:

- **Report on Carcinogens:** The NTP prepares the RoC in response to a requirement that the Secretary of the Department of Health and Human Services publish a biennial report that contains a list of known or reasonably anticipated carcinogens and information concerning the public's exposure to these substances. The Secretary delegated responsibility for preparing the RoC to the NTP. The RoC identifies and characterizes cancer hazards for the federal government for use by the American people. The RoC is a science-based, public health report that identifies agents, substances, mixtures, or exposures in the environment that may potentially put people in the United States at increased risk for cancer. The RoC contains qualitative information gathered from available sources, including cancer studies on humans, animals and on possible mechanisms of action; potential sources of exposure to humans; and current federal regulations to limit exposures. Substances are listed in the report as either known or reasonably anticipated human carcinogens.
- **HAT Monographs:** In addition to the RoC toxicity assessments, the NTP issues OHAT Monographs. The OHAT conducts evaluations to

assess the evidence that environmental chemicals, physical substances, or mixtures (collectively referred to as "substances") cause adverse health effects and provides opinions on whether these substances may be of concern given what is known about current human exposure levels. The OHAT also organizes workshops or state-of-the-science evaluations to address issues of importance in environmental health sciences.

- **Tox21:** NTP coordinates with several other agencies on another toxicity assessment activity called Tox21.[34] Tox21 pools federal resources and expertise from EPA, NTP, the National Institutes of Health, and the Food and Drug Administration. According to NTP, among the goals of Tox21 are to research, develop, validate, and translate innovative chemical testing methods that characterize toxicity pathways, to prioritize which chemicals need more extensive toxicological evaluation, and to develop models that can be used to more effectively predict how chemicals will affect biological responses.

OSHA

OSHA is an agency within the Department of Labor that conducts chemical toxicity assessments as part of its regulatory responsibilities to promulgate and enforce mandatory occupational safety and health standards. OSHA, created by the Occupational Safety and Health Act of 1970,[35] has the authority to set standards for toxic chemicals, including permissible exposure limits (PEL), which adequately assure to the extent feasible, on the basis of the best available evidence, that no employee will suffer material impairment of health or functional capacity even if the employee has regular exposure during his or her working life.[36] Standards must be reasonably necessary or appropriate, meaning that, before issuing a standard, OSHA must demonstrate that the chemical involved poses a significant risk under workplace conditions permitted by current regulations and that the new limit OSHA promulgates will substantially reduce that risk. Moreover, the standard must be technologically and economically feasible, better able to effectuate the purposes of the OSH Act than any relevant national consensus standards, and use the most cost-effective protective measures.[37] OSHA's analysis includes both qualitative and quantitative components and evaluates the scientific evidence linking exposure to a variety of adverse health effects, including both chronic disease (such as cancer) and effects that may occur over a shorter term.

OSHA health standards are usually directed at reducing the risk of workers developing diseases from occupational exposure to hazardous chemicals. According to OSHA officials, before it issues a health regulation, OSHA reviews the best available evidence pertaining to the adverse health effects of exposure, and evaluates the risk of these effects from exposures allowed under the current standard, as well as the expected impact of the new or revised standard on risk. OSHA officials noted that, because the process of promulgating health standards is resource-intensive and time-consuming, the number of toxicity assessments performed by the agency is limited. Its last two risk assessments conducted as part of its regulatory responsibilities in issuing proposed and final rules were hexavalent chromium, which was proposed in 2004 and finalized in 2006, and crystalline silica, which was proposed in 2013. OSHA noted that another analysis is planned for beryllium.[38]

OSHA's determination of the effects an occupational exposure causes, and which of these effects cause material impairment, is primarily qualitative and relies on evaluation of research conducted by a wide variety of outside organizations, both governmental (such as NIOSH) and nongovernmental. Once OSHA has identified the health effects of concern, the agency conducts an assessment to determine whether longterm exposure at the current PEL would pose a significant risk to workers' health, and whether adoption of a new PEL will substantially reduce this risk. This analysis includes both qualitative and quantitative components. The determination that a particular level of risk is significant is a policy and legal determination, rather than a scientific determination. OSHA also must show, among other things, that a new PEL is technologically and economically feasible.[39]

NIOSH

NIOSH, an Institute of the Centers for Disease Control and Prevention, develops toxicity assessments of workplace chemicals and develops recommended standards for them under the authority of the Occupational Safety and Health Act of 1970.[40] NIOSH develops criteria for a recommended standard, including recommended exposure limits (REL)[41] to describe levels at which no employee will suffer impaired health or functional capacities or diminished life expectancy as a result of his or her work experience.[42] NIOSH publishes chemical assessment information and recommendations for preventing exposure in documents that may contain quantitative or qualitative assessment information on the cancer or noncancer effects of chemicals.

NIOSH officials told us that REL development is a resource-intensive process involving comprehensive review of the scientific literature, statistical modeling that includes sensitivity analyses, and discussion of the health effects of the chemical and the risk assessment process. To date, the NIOSH Pocket Guide to Chemical Hazards lists 677 chemicals or substance groupings, some with NIOSH RELs, 135 of which are carcinogens.[43] In recent years, NIOSH has conducted quantitative risk assessments as the basis of RELs. NIOSH also recommends appropriate preventive measures to reduce or eliminate the adverse health effects of workplace chemicals of concern. These recommendations are then published for consideration by OSHA for use in promulgating legal standards.[44]

NIOSH assessments are designed to address occupational hazards and risks to workers rather than environmental hazards and risks to the general public. Therefore the most relevant data and results of occupational assessments may differ from those developed to identify environmental hazards and risks to the general public because the population being assessed—workers— does not include young children and has fewer elderly or infirm individuals. NIOSH occupational assessments also consider exposure over a working lifetime—40-hour workweek, 52 weeks per year for 45 years—as opposed to continuous environmental exposure.

NIOSH officials told us they use the best available data as the basis for quantitative risk assessments. These data may be from epidemiological studies, experimental animal studies, and/or mechanistic data in the scientific literature. Because NIOSH has statutory access to workplaces, many NIOSH assessments have also been based on epidemiological investigations of workplace exposures. When NIOSH conducts quantitative assessment using published laboratory animal data for extrapolation to humans, the human equivalent dose associated with an adverse effect is calculated from animal data, and risk is extrapolated to a working lifetime concentration.

Selected States Largely Rely on Federal Chemical Toxicity Assessments

Officials from the 10 selected states that we reviewed generally do not produce their own chemical toxicity assessments; instead, they generally rely on federal chemical toxicity assessments. Officials from 6 of the 10 states we reviewed—Alaska, Arizona, Delaware, Missouri, New York, Oklahoma—told us they have limited resources and relied on chemical toxicity assessments produced by federal agencies. Officials from the remaining 4—California, Minnesota, New Jersey, and Texas—told us they sometimes produce their own chemical toxicity assessment information, but they more often rely on federal sources. Officials in all 10 states told us that they have used data in the last 5 years from some or all of the five federal agencies we reviewed.

Officials from California, Minnesota, New Jersey, and Texas told us that although they have the expertise and the resources to produce their own toxicity assessments, they still rely on data from federal agencies. For example, an official from California told us that although the state has the capacity to develop its own toxicity assessments, state officials still regularly consult sources from the five federal agencies we reviewed. Officials from Minnesota told us they evaluate existing sources of toxicity information and sometimes recommend that an existing toxicity standard be used while they evaluate the adequacy of that standard and whether acceptable methods were used in deriving it. They also told us they have the capability to develop hazard identification and dose response analyses that may then be used to evaluate an exposure and set new standards if necessary.

An official from New Jersey told us the state reviews the existing scientific literature for each chemical and, if it determines that the existing toxicity assessments—often provided by a federal agency—meet its needs, it uses them; otherwise, it develops its own. The official told us the state may also develop toxicity assessments for chemicals that are not national priorities, meaning that no federal agency is currently reviewing them. For example, this New Jersey official told us the state developed an assessment for MTBE, a chemical that it indicated was a huge problem for many states and for which IRIS did not have a toxicity value.[45]

An official from Texas told us the state considers several factors in deciding whether to develop its own toxicity values. These factors include whether a toxicity value is available; the age of existing toxicity values; the frequency with which a particular chemical occurs in Texas; whether it disagrees with the scientific judgment used to derive the toxicity value; and public input or concern about a particular chemical.

Selected Federal Agencies' Chemical Toxicity Assessment Activities Are Fragmented and Overlapping but Are Not Duplicative

The chemical toxicity assessment activities at the five federal agencies we reviewed are fragmented because they address the same broad area of national need; they overlap because they have similar goals, and some target similar beneficiaries. We did not find evidence that the activities at these agencies are duplicative because they do not engage in the same activities or provide the same services to the same beneficiaries.

Fragmentation

Selected federal agencies' chemical toxicity assessment activities are fragmented because they each address the same broad area of national need—providing information on the toxicity of chemicals. However, while these federal agencies' all provide information on this same broad area, their activities differ in type and purpose. For example, although both OSHA and EPA develop chemical toxicity assessment information, OSHA provides information on occupational hazards that affect workers, while EPA provides information on environmental hazards that affect the broader population, including children and the elderly. Also, the duration and routes of exposure that are of interest to EPA and OSHA may differ. For example, EPA's IRIS Program assesses the effects of lifetime or chronic exposure to a chemical in the environment, and OSHA assesses the effects of occupational exposure to a chemical in the workplace over a working lifetime, as well as shorter term exposures. For example, EPA's toxicity value for the chemical acrolein differs from OSHA's values because EPA's value is for chronic exposure in the environment, and OSHA's two toxicity values are for 15-minute and 8-hour exposures in the workplace, respectively (see app. II, which contains a table of chemical toxicity values compared across four of the five selected federal agencies and 1 of the 12 selected state agencies). According to OSHA officials, OSHA is primarily concerned with exposure through dermal (skin) contact or inhalation. According to EPA officials, several EPA Offices are concerned with all routes of exposure (dermal, inhalation, and ingestion) for workers and the broader population.

We have previously reported on instances of fragmentation in the federal government. For example, in April 2014,[46] we concluded that fragmentation may result in inefficiencies in how the government delivers services. In March 2011,[47] we also reported that fragmentation has the potential to result in duplication of resources. However, in our April 2014 report, we also found that fragmentation is, by itself, not an indication that unnecessary duplication of efforts or activities exists. For chemical toxicity assessments, we did not find evidence that their activities were duplicative. For example, NTP provides qualitative information to the public on chemicals in the environment known to be or reasonably anticipated to be human carcinogens in its RoC. In contrast, NIOSH provides quantitative and qualitative information to OSHA to support legal standards on both carcinogenic and noncarcinogenic effects of workplace chemicals in its policy documents, which is summarized in the NIOSH Pocket Guide to Chemical Hazards.

In our March 2011 report, we also stated that there can be advantages to having multiple federal agencies involved in a broad area of national need. Agencies can tailor initiatives to suit their specific missions and needs, among other things. For example, OSHA primarily focuses on occupational health issues that affect working-aged adults exposed over an 8-hour workday, and ATSDR is required to focus on environmental health issues that affect the broader population, including children, the elderly, and pregnant women, who may be exposed over longer time periods. In addition, ATSDR has developed three toxicity values for the chemical 1,4-dioxane, a solvent, for nonoccupational environmental exposures (see app. II). These toxicity values differ from OSHA's toxicity value for the same chemical, which is intended only for exposure in the workplace.[48]

Overlap

Selected federal agencies' chemical toxicity assessment activities overlap because some of these activities have similar goals—such as identifying the extent to which a chemical may cause cancer—and because some target similar beneficiaries—such as local health authorities for use in dealing with hazardous waste sites or the general public. However, in March 2011,[49] we concluded that overlapping programs may be aligned in a way that they are complementary. For example, NIOSH toxicity assessments are designed to address occupational hazards and the risks to workers, rather than environmental hazards and the risks to the general public that ATSDR assesses. The population being assessed for occupational risks includes workers who represent a subset of the general public, and it does not include young children and has fewer elderly or infirm individuals. For example, NIOSH developed two toxicity values for the chemical carbon disulfide, a solvent, for workplace exposures, and other agencies, such as ATSDR, developed its toxicity value for environmental exposure that affects the general public (see app. II). NIOSH occupational assessments also consider exposure over a working lifetime—a 40-hour workweek, 52 weeks per year for 45 years— as opposed to continuous environmental exposure.

Selected federal agencies' chemical toxicity assessment activities also overlap in that some of these agencies target similar beneficiaries. For example, both EPA IRIS assessments and ATSDR toxicological profiles are used by a broad audience, including the general public, academics, and international groups. However, beneficiaries for these agencies also differ. EPA's IRIS program provides scientifically supported toxicity values for EPA's program offices and regions for the purpose of making regulatory and risk management decisions, and ATSDR's toxicological profiles target local health authorities for use in dealing with hazardous waste sites. We have previously concluded that overlapping programs or activities can be a harbinger of unnecessary duplication.[50] However, in this case, because these federal agencies develop distinct chemical toxicity assessment information, their activities are largely complementary. For example, as noted previously in this report in Figure 3, all five selected federal agencies' activities overlap in that they provide information on both cancer and noncancer effects. However, as previously noted, OSHA provides information on occupational hazards that affect workers, and EPA provides information on the environmental hazards that affect the broader population, including children or the elderly. Further, we have previously concluded that funding research on the same topic may be appropriate and necessary—for example, for purposes of replicating or corroborating results.[51] Likewise, officials from two of the five selected federal agencies we reviewed similarly told us that scientific findings are more robust if more than one agency has studied the same chemical and arrived at similar results.

Duplication

We did not find evidence of duplication among selected federal agencies' chemical toxicity assessment activities because the agencies did not engage in the same activities or provide the same services to the same beneficiaries. For example, we did not find duplication between NIOSH and EPA's chemical toxicity assessment activities because NIOSH assesses the potential risks that chemicals pose to working-aged adults in occupational settings (e.g., exposure by dermal contact or inhalation) over the course of working time periods (e.g., an 8- or 10-hour workday or a 40-hour workweek). In contrast, EPA assesses risks that chemicals pose to a broader population as opposed to workers, which includes children and vulnerable populations in the larger nonoccupational environment (e.g., in the air, soil, or groundwater) typically over the course of an entire lifetime.[52] Such differences in the health and age of the people exposed, the environment in which the chemical is present, the routes in which the chemical comes into contact with people, and the length of time people are exposed affect the chemical toxicity information the agencies produce about the levels at which a chemical is safe.

In addition, in reviewing examples of such chemical toxicity information, we analyzed 10 selected chemicals' inhalation toxicity values for four of the five selected federal agencies and 1 of the 12 selected state agencies. We found that these values are not duplicative because they are (1) based on different chemical toxicity assessment activities of differing exposure durations and (2) fulfill distinct programmatic and statutory requirements. For example, EPA and NIOSH developed different toxicity values for the chemical hexavalent chromium,[53] but EPA's values were for chronic exposure, and NIOSH's value was for a 40-hour per week working lifetime exposure (see app. II). Also, EPA and NIOSH's values each responded to a need from different beneficiaries. Specifically, EPA developed the values in response to stakeholder chemical nominations to the IRIS program,[54] and NIOSH developed the value as part of its responsibilities under the Occupational Safety and Health Act. In addition, as previously noted, both NTP and EPA assess the potential for chemicals to cause cancer and noncancer health effects. According to an NTP official, the agency describes such potential to the public in a qualitative manner based on a targeted population (e.g., pregnant woman), and EPA does so in a qualitative and quantitative manner, consistent with data available for the broader population that includes all subsets (e.g., healthy adults, children, the elderly).

Selected Federal Agencies and States Coordinate Their Chemical Toxicity Assessment Activities and Reported Cross-Cutting Challenges

Officials from all five of the federal agencies and from 3 of the 10 states we reviewed told us that they coordinate their chemical toxicity assessment activities. All of the five federal agencies we reviewed have coordinated with other agencies in the last 5 years, and all the states we reviewed have used federal assessment information, and some have coordinated with federal agencies in the last 5 years. In addition, both officials from selected federal agencies and states identified cross-cutting challenges to this coordination, such as constraints on sharing confidential business information and reliance on informal communication processes.

Selected Federal Agencies and States Coordinate Their Chemical Toxicity Assessment Activities

Officials at all five of the federal agencies and 3 of the 10 states we reviewed told us that, in the last 5 years, they have coordinated their chemical toxicity assessment activities using a variety of coordination mechanisms. We found that all of the federal agencies we reviewed have coordinated with one another, and that states largely rely on federal chemical toxicity assessment information.

Federal Coordination

Agency officials at the five federal agencies we reviewed told us they have coordinated their chemical toxicity assessment activities in the last 5 years by using four mechanisms: (1) memorandums of understanding (MOU); (2) interagency working groups; (3) data sharing, such as literature search results; and (4) chemical-specific coordination on an as-needed basis, meaning the agencies coordinate in an informal fashion as the need arises for particular chemicals.[55] According to our analysis of structured interviews with selected federal agencies, all five federal agencies have coordinated with at least three other federal agencies using at least three of the four mechanisms (see Figure 4).

Agency officials told us that these interactions have had a positive effect on their chemical toxicity assessment activities. For example:

- ATSDR and EPA coordinate their chemical toxicity assessment activities though an MOU established in 2004 and renewed in 2013. Specifically, ATSDR and EPA's National Center for Environmental Assessment, within its Office of Research and Development, entered into the MOU with a stated purpose of (1) identifying chemical-specific priorities of mutual interest; (2) identifying potential points of interaction that will provide opportunities for collaboration; (3) harmonizing assessment approaches for chemicals of public health concern; (4) increasing the pool of available scientific expertise; and (5) avoiding duplication of effort. Examples of coordination under this MOU include sharing information on chemicals of concern and reviewing and commenting on draft assessments. An EPA official also noted that this MOU enables the agencies to share chemical nomination proposals for their respective programs—ATSDR toxicological profiles and EPA IRIS assessments—and discuss any overlap in chemicals they are assessing.

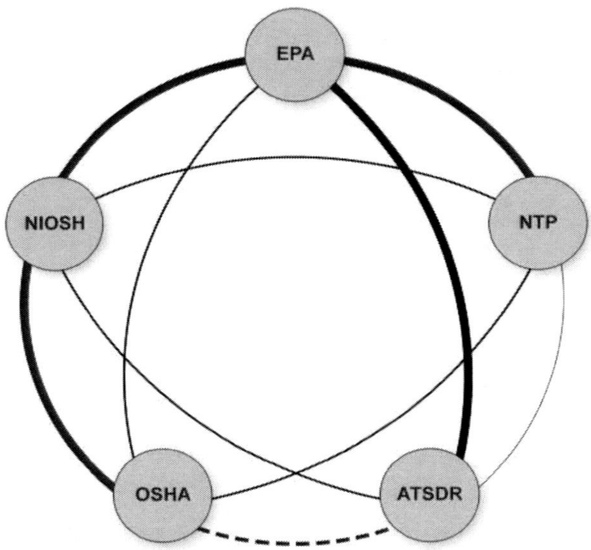

Signifies the agency pair coordinates using all four mechanisms:

1. memorandum of understanding
2. interagency working group
3. data sharing, such as literature search results
4. chemical-specific coordination on an as-needed basis

Signifies the agency pair coordinates using the three mechanisms below, but not the memorandum of understanding:

1. interagency working group
2. data sharing, such as literature search results
3. chemical-specific coordination on an as-needed basis

Signifies the agency pair coordinates using the one mechanism below:

1. interagency working group

For example, ATSDR coordinates with NTP, EPA, NIOSH, and OSHA. The coordination between ATSDR and EPA involves the use of all four mechanisms and is indicated by a thick line.

Abbreviations:

ATSDR Agency for Toxic Substances and Disease Registry
EPA Environmental Protection Agency
NIOSH National Institute for Occupational Safety and Health
NTP National Toxicology Program
OSHA Occupational Safety and Health Administration

Source: GAO analysis of data obtained from structured interviews with federal officials. | GAO-14-763.

Figure 4. Coordination between Selected Federal Agencies on Chemical Toxicity Assessment Activities.

- OSHA and NIOSH have frequently coordinated on chemical toxicity assessment activities for a number of years by sharing information and data pertaining to emerging occupational safety and health issues; sharing information related to assessment methods, tools, databases and data analysis; and developing and disseminating collaborative and joint-publications in areas of mutual interest. In 2014, OSHA and NIOSH entered into an MOU that formalized these coordination activities and has a stated purpose of advancing the protection of workers, promoting best practices, and encouraging employers to develop and utilize safety and health management programs and effective prevention strategies and technologies.
- NTP coordinates with many federal agencies through its Executive Committee, which is an interagency advisory group that provides programmatic and policy oversight to the NTP Director and meets once or twice a year with high-ranking members from the other four selected federal agencies, as well as other federal agencies. The purpose of the Executive Committee is focused on advising on NTP activities and policies, but NTP officials told us that the Executive Committee has also addressed cross-cutting issues related to chemical toxicity assessments that are beyond a single agency's ability to solve, such as facilitating a forum for ATSDR, NIOSH, and OSHA to present updates of their assessment activities to the other Executive Committee member agencies; explore interests, needs, and capabilities among member agencies; and identify ways for enhanced cooperation. In another Executive Committee meeting, member agencies discussed efforts within the federal government to adopt the Globally Harmonized System of Classification and Labeling of Chemicals, which includes criteria for the classification of health, physical, and environmental hazards, as well as specifying what information should be included on labels and safety information sheets of hazardous chemicals. NTP officials stated that the agency was interested to hear about agencies' plans for implementation in regulatory programs and how NTP products would be used in the context of the system.

Agencies also provided examples of how they have coordinated through such mechanisms as sharing data and coordinating on specific chemicals on an as-needed basis. For example:

- According to an OSHA official, OSHA shares information informally with EPA and other federal agencies to discuss ongoing research efforts within federal agencies and the current state of science on nanomaterials.[56] Specifically, the OSHA official stated that the agencies are examining the data on specific nanomaterials, such as nanosilver, which, according to EPA, has been incorporated into a variety of consumer products due to their antimicrobial properties, such as some soaps, disinfectant sprays, and children's toys. The OSHA official stated that the agencies are reviewing current scientific data and sharing information on how this type of data can be used by regulatory agencies.
- An ATSDR official stated that ATSDR sometimes refers to EPA's quantitative toxicity assessment information in developing new or updating MRLs. For instance, ATSDR is adopting EPA's chronic toxicity values for trichloroethylene (TCE), which is used as a solvent in industrial degreasing operations, and is also used in consumer products such as typewriter correction fluids, paint removers and strippers, adhesives, spot removers, and rug-cleaning fluids. For more information on toxicity values for TCE across selected agencies, please see appendix II.
- An NTP official stated that NTP is working toward sharing data with EPA, such as literature searches on chemicals. The official also stated that, as part of its systematic review process, NTP is developing web-based tools that would allow all federal agencies to extract data from literature, assess the quality of that study, and choose studies for a toxicity assessment in a consistent and structured way. This tool is being funded by EPA, and earlier iterations of these tools have been used in the ongoing EPA assessment of arsenic.

State Use of Federal Chemical Toxicity Assessment Information and Coordination

Officials in the 10 states we reviewed told us that they largely rely on federal agency chemical toxicity assessments. Specifically, officials from agencies in all 10 of the states we reviewed told us they have used chemical toxicity assessment information produced by the federal agencies we reviewed in the last 5 years, even if they had developed their own assessments.[57] Officials from 6 of the 10 states we reviewed— Arizona, California, Delaware, Minnesota, Oklahoma, and Texas— responded that they had used data from all five federal agencies. Officials in the other four states—Missouri, Alaska,

New Jersey, and New York— responded that they had used chemical toxicity assessment information from two to four of the five federal agencies (see Figure 5).

We also asked officials in the 10 selected states we reviewed whether they had coordinated with federal agencies through mechanisms such as MOUs, interagency working groups, data sharing, or chemical-specific coordination on an as-needed basis. Officials in 3 of the 10 states we reviewed—Alaska, Minnesota, and Oklahoma—responded that they have coordinated with three out of the five selected federal agencies in the last 5 years. For example, officials in Minnesota responded that the state has coordinated with ATSDR, EPA, and NTP; officials in Oklahoma responded that the state has coordinated with EPA. An official from the Alaska Department of Environmental Conservation, which does not produce its own chemical toxicity assessments, stated that it coordinated with ATSDR and EPA to assess a chemical contaminating drinking water. The chemical, sulfolane, is an industrial solvent used to separate compounds from chemical mixtures and, according to the Alaska Department, has been the primary solvent used at the North Pole Refinery since 1985. In 2009, then-owner Flint Hills found that sulfolane levels in nearby private drinking water wells were significantly higher than expected, although under the state standard that requires cleanup.

Because there was little toxicity assessment information available on sulfolane, the Alaska Department contacted EPA; at the same time, the state health department contacted ATSDR, resulting in the group of agencies working together to assess the chemical. ATSDR conducted evaluations in 2010 and 2011 that resulted in the establishment of a stricter cleanup standard. After considering ATSDR's research and its own research on previously published data, EPA established a PPRTV for sulfolane in 2012. The state of Alaska set a stricter groundwater cleanup standard based on this PPRTV. The Alaska official we interviewed stated that Alaska lacked the necessary resources to assess sulfolane on its own and working with EPA and ATSDR provided the state with information it needed to move forward on a remediation plan.

	Federal agency				
	Agency for Toxic Substances and Disease Registry	Environmental Protection Agency	National Institute for Occupational Safety and health	National Toxicology Program	Occupational Safety and Health Administration
Alaska	●	●		●	
Arizona	●	●	●	●	●
California	●	●	●	●	●
Delaware	●	●	●	●	●
Minnesota	●	●	●	●	●
Missouri	●	●	●		●
New Jersey	●	●		●	
New York	●	●			
Oklahoma	●	●	●	●	●
Texas	●	●	●	●	●

● State agency reported use of federal agency chemical toxicity assessment information

(shaded) GAO spoke with two agencies within this state and aggregated their responses

Source: GAO analysis of data obtained from structured interviews with state officials. | GAO-14-763.

Figure 5. State-Reported Use of Federal Agency Chemical Toxicity Assessment Information.

Officials from three states we reviewed told us that they coordinated with federal agencies, and officials from all five selected federal agencies told us they coordinated with a variety of state agencies. For example:

- An EPA official stated that its NCEA office operates the Superfund Technical Support Center, which provides assessment technical support and advice to EPA program and regional offices and states on an as-needed basis. The EPA official said that, over the last 5 years, 20 states called the center through a publicly available hotline for information on topics related to chemical risk assessments.
- Officials from ATSDR stated that the agency does not formally coordinate with states, but that states often provide comments during its public comment period on toxicological profiles. Also, ATSDR officials stated that the agency has used state chemical toxicity assessment information to develop its toxicological profiles.
- Officials from OSHA stated that their largest coordination effort with states is through NIOSH's Adult Blood Lead Epidemiology and Surveillance state program, a program funded through NIOSH in which 41 states collect data on levels of blood lead levels. The participating states provide data to NIOSH, which then publishes the data and makes them available in summary form to OSHA. OSHA uses the data to help target workplace inspections and other consultations designed to reduce exposures to lead in the workplace.

Officials from some agencies from selected states responded to our structured interviews that they also coordinate with other states on chemical toxicity assessment activities. Officials from 4 of the 10 selected states—Arizona, Minnesota, Missouri, and New Jersey—told us that they coordinated with other states. For example, officials from the Minnesota Department of Health told us that it is a member of the Federal-State Toxicology Risk Analysis Committee (FSTRAC), an interagency working group led by EPA's Office of Water that includes other states and whose stated purpose is to foster cooperation, consistency, and an understanding of EPA's and different states' goals and problems in human health risk assessment.

Selected Federal Agencies and States Identified Cross-Cutting Challenges to Coordination

Officials from three of the five selected federal agencies and 2 of the 10 selected states we reviewed identified three cross-cutting challenges to coordination on chemical toxicity assessment activities, including the following:

- **Constraints on sharing confidential business information**. Officials from three offices within EPA we reviewed told us that they are limited in how they can share proprietary information about business practices that chemical companies identify as confidential business information (CBI). Because of legal restrictions on dissemination of CBI, it cannot readily be shared across agencies, which hinders the agencies' coordination of chemical toxicity assessment activities. For example, one official stated that each agency and offices within agencies operate under laws that contain varying provisions relating to CBI, and that these varying provisions complicate their ability to share scientific data and can even make data sharing impossible. This official also stated that these varying provisions hinder their ability to leverage resources. As we concluded in March 2013,[58] when information is claimed as CBI, it limits EPA's ability to share it with other entities, which potentially limits the effectiveness of these organizations' environmental risk programs.[59] However, TSCA specifies when EPA may publicly disclose chemical information it obtains from chemical companies and provides that chemical companies can claim certain information, such as data disclosing chemical processes, as CBI.[60] We also reported in March 2013 that, according to EPA, 95 percent of information the agency receives on new chemicals contains assertions of confidentiality. EPA officials have stated that they have not had the resources that would be needed to investigate and, as appropriate, challenge such claims.
- **Limited opportunities for agency officials to meet.** According to officials from ATSDR, NIOSH, EPA, and two states, there are few opportunities to meet face-to-face among counterparts from federal and state agencies because budgetary challenges limit their ability to host or attend conferences. For example, one state official noted that in-person conferences were useful because there were opportunities to have spontaneous conversations and establish relationships with their

state and federal peers. Due to budget restrictions, however, federal agencies have moved toward hosting webinars instead, which the both federal and state agency officials told us allowed them to share information between state and federal agencies on their assessment activities without the costs associated with traveling, but did not provide the same opportunities for coordination and networking. Officials from one federal agency and one state told us that webinars may preclude the kind of networking that happens at in-person conferences.

- **Informal communication processes**. Officials from NIOSH and three EPA offices told us that they believe that points of contact and communication processes are too informal. For example, one federal agency official stated that there may not be an identified point of contact when individuals retire or leave for another position, which can contribute to loss of continuity and disrupt the transfer of knowledge between agencies if retiring individuals depart without a process for ensuring a smooth transition of knowledge from incumbents to successors. Another federal official stated that an individual in the same position for decades may build relationships with officials in other agencies, but that, without systematic and routine mechanisms to coordinate, it would be challenging for a new individual to identify the right points of contact—particularly at state and regional government agencies. We previously concluded in November 2010 that by using informal coordination mechanisms, agencies may rely on relationships with individual officials to ensure effective collaboration and that these informal relationships could end once personnel move to their next assignments.[61] We also concluded that agencies can strengthen their commitment to work collaboratively by articulating their roles and responsibilities to facilitate decision making in formal documents such as MOUs, interagency guidance, or interagency planning documents.

The National Science and Technology Council Offers an Opportunity to Address Cross-Cutting Challenges

In our September 2012 report that identified mechanisms that facilitate interagency collaboration, we found one mechanism for addressing cross-cutting challenges is through an existing interagency working group.[62] In that report, we concluded that interagency mechanisms or strategies to coordinate programs that address cross-cutting issues may reduce potentially duplicative, overlapping, and fragmented efforts. Officials from four federal agencies told us that one such group that all five selected federal agencies participate in is the National Science and Technology Council (NSTC). NSTC, which was established by Executive Order in 1993, is a council of cabinet-level officials chaired by the President and managed by the Director of the Office of Science and Technology Policy (OSTP).[63] NSTC has multiple committees addressing its broad responsibilities for the scientific and technical work of the executive branch. For example, the NSTC's Committee on Environment, Natural Resources, and Sustainability advises and assists NSTC on federal research and development related to the environment, natural resources, and sustainability. According to the NSTC Executive Order, its principal functions are to coordinate the science and technology policymaking process and ensure science and technology are considered in development and implementation of federal policies and programs, among other things. Further, all executive departments and agencies, whether or not they are represented on the NSTC, are to coordinate science and technology policy through the NSTC and share information on research and development budget requests.

We noted the value of the NSTC in our May 2012 report on a federal interagency program on nanotechnology, in which we stated that the NSTC is the principal means by which the executive branch coordinates science and technology policy.[64] In August 2011, we also reported that one of NSTC's workgroups was involved in another interagency effort to identify and prioritize research needed to better understand pharmaceuticals in the environment and recommend areas of federal collaboration to address those priorities.[65] A July 2014 NSTC report on data from observations of the Earth, such as its land surface and oceans, also illustrates NSTC's involvement in coordinating science activities across agencies. The report was produced as a result of a statutory requirement that OSTP establish a mechanism to ensure greater coordination of research, operations, and activities relating to civilian Earth observation. In response, OSTP convened a task force of 15 federal agencies, and subsequently, the NSTC published the 2014 report. Senior officials from three agencies—ATDSR, EPA, and NIOSH— identified a committee within NSTC as an appropriate forum to address such challenges. An official from OSTP similarly stated that NSTC could serve an interagency coordinating function to address certain crosscutting challenges, and it has already done so by coordinating chemical toxicity assessment activities and providing opportunities for agency officials to meet in person. By having an interagency body to address the challenges the five selected agencies identified (i.e., constraints on sharing CBI, limited opportunities for agency officials to meet, and informal communication processes) and any future cross-cutting challenges, the five agencies would be positioned to better coordinate their assessment activities in the most effective and efficient manner.

CONCLUSION

With thousands of chemicals in commercial use in the United States, decision makers rely on information derived from toxicity assessment to examine the risks these substances may pose. Using various mechanisms, the federal agencies and some of the state agencies we reviewed actively coordinate their toxicity assessment activities to avoid unnecessary fragmentation, overlap, and duplication. However, officials in states and federal agencies identified cross-cutting challenges to coordination, such as constraints on sharing information and informal communication processes that hinder agencies' ability to leverage resources, and interfere with officials' ability to work across agency boundaries. By addressing these cross-cutting challenges, state and federal agencies may be positioned to more effectively and efficiently coordinate their chemical toxicity assessment activities.

RECOMMENDATION FOR EXECUTIVE ACTION

To improve coordination of federal and state chemical toxicity assessment activities, we recommend that the Director of OSTP encourage the NSTC to support relevant federal agency officials' efforts to address, as appropriate, the agencies' cross-cutting coordination challenges, such as constraints on sharing confidential business information, limited opportunities for agency officials to meet, and informal communication processes.

AGENCY COMMENTS AND OUR EVALUATION

We requested comments on a draft of this report from the Director, Office of Science and Technology Policy; Secretary of Health and Human Services; Secretary of Labor; and Administrator, Environmental Protection Agency.

They did not provide official written comments to include in our report. Instead, they provided technical comments, which we incorporated as appropriate.

Steve D. Morris
Acting Director,
Natural Resources and Environment Team

APPENDIX I: SCOPE AND METHODOLOGY

To describe the chemical toxicity assessment activities selected federal and state agencies undertake, we examined the chemical toxicity assessment activities of five federal agencies: (1) the Agency for Toxic Substances and Disease Registry (ATSDR), (2) the Environmental Protection Agency (EPA), (3) the National Institute for Occupational Safety and Health (NIOSH), (4) the National Toxicology Program (NTP), and (5) the Occupational Safety and Health Administration (OSHA), which follow the National Academies' four-step risk assessment process. The four steps are (1) hazard identification, (2) dose-response assessment, (3) exposure assessment, and (4) risk characterization.[1] The first two steps—hazard identification and dose-response assessment—are commonly referred to together as toxicity assessments. We reviewed publicly available information on these five federal agencies' assessment activities and information from our past reports, and compiled summaries of these activities for each agency. We then submitted these summaries to each agency to review for accuracy and incorporated their comments as appropriate. We also interviewed agency officials as necessary to clarify their comments. We selected a nonprobability sample of 12 state agencies in 10 states that provide a range of chemical toxicity assessment activities.[2] An official from the Interstate Technology & Regulatory Council (ITRC)—an organization which has expertise in the area of state chemical toxicity assessment activities—reviewed our questions before we interviewed agency officials, and we made changes as appropriate.[3] We asked officials from each state agency to describe the activities their agency performs that might be included in those first two steps of a risk assessment (hazard identification and dose-response), to describe what is within its agency's purview as opposed to the purview of another agency within the same state, and whether it has developed its own chemical toxicity assessment information in the last 5 years. We asked officials from each state agency whether their agency had referred to existing assessment information from each of the five selected federal agencies in the last 5 years, among other entities. Because this was a nonprobability sample, the information and perspectives that we obtained from these state agencies are not generalizable to other state agencies. A contractor entered all agencies' quantitative responses into a single spreadsheet, and their qualitative responses into a single document. We then analyzed responses from our interviews about the extent to which state agencies had developed their own chemical toxicity assessments in the last 5 years, and the extent to which the agencies had used chemical toxicity assessment information from the five federal agencies in the last 5 years.

To assess the extent to which, if at all, selected federal agencies' chemical toxicity assessment activities are fragmented, overlapping, or duplicative, we reviewed the summaries of federal agency assessment activities and federal agency documentation that sets forth the scope and purpose of their assessment activities, and we compared them with one another and with our definitions of fragmentation, overlap, and duplication. We also asked the five federal agencies in our structured interviews whether consolidation—a response to duplication that involves a reduction in either physical infrastructure or management functions—of their agency's chemical toxicity assessment activities with those of the other four federal agencies could improve the federal government's chemical toxicity assessment activities. In addition, we spoke with industry and environmental groups to hear their perspective on the chemical toxicity assessment activities of the five federal agencies and state agencies and, the extent to which, if at all, they are duplicative. We also further reviewed a nonprobability sample of inhalation toxicity values for 10 selected chemicals as developed by four of the five federal agencies (ATSDR, EPA, NIOSH, and OSHA) and one state agency, the California Environmental Protection Agency (CalEPA), that conduct toxicity assessment activities for these inhaled chemicals.[4] We illustrated the differences in reported toxicity values in each agency but did not evaluate the validity of these levels or the methods by which they were developed. Because this was a nonprobability sample, the information that we obtained on these 10 chemicals is not generalizable to all chemicals. We did not include NTP among the federal agencies because it does not develop quantitative toxicity values. We included CalEPA to provide an illustrative example of a state's toxicity values. We selected these 10 chemicals to provide a diverse range of organic and inorganic chemicals—the two major categories that comprise the universe of all chemicals—with varying structures and chemical properties, which we identified with the assistance of a GAO chemist and a review of chemical toxicity values from federal agencies. We limited our sample to chemicals for which all of the four of the five selected federal agencies and 1 of the 12 selected state agencies had developed toxicity values.

To examine federal and state agencies' coordination on chemical toxicity assessment activities and any challenges associated in doing so, we administered structured interviews to the five selected federal agencies and 12 state agencies. For EPA, which unlike most of the other federal and state agencies has multiple components that conduct chemical toxicity assessments, we also interviewed officials from six program or regional offices to determine the extent to which they coordinate their toxicity assessment activities and identify any challenges to their efforts.[5] We spoke with officials in two agencies within both Delaware and Minnesota because state officials from these two states indicated that chemical toxicity assessment responsibilities were split among different agencies within their states. In our interviews, we asked officials from each of the five federal agencies whether their agency had coordinated with each of the other four federal agencies within the past 5 years. For each federal agency that it said it had coordinated with, we asked whether it had used each of five mechanisms: (1) memorandums of understanding (MOU); (2) interagency working groups; (3) data sharing, such as literature search results; (4) chemical-specific coordination on an as-needed basis; and (5) other mechanisms. For each of the mechanisms they said they had used, we asked whether and in what ways the mechanism helped the agency to effectively produce chemical toxicity assessments. For each of the mechanisms they said they did not use, we asked whether they thought that the use of the mechanism would improve the federal government's chemical toxicity assessments. We asked a similar set of questions about each federal agency's coordination with states; we also asked a similar set of questions about each of the 12 selected state agencies' coordination with the five selected federal agencies and other states.[6] We analyzed and reported interview responses using the state as the unit of measure, as opposed to the particular agency. Because we used the state as the unit of measure and not the agency, we reported the response as "yes" for a state in cases where at least one agency official or one agency within Delaware or Minnesota responded "yes." Where applicable, we corroborated coordination activities by obtaining signed MOUs and written interagency agreements. The different mechanisms through which agencies coordinate do not necessarily indicate better quality or more effective coordination. Whether the type of coordination mechanism affected quality of effectiveness is beyond the scope of this review. We combined federal agency responses into an analysis performed by GAO methodologists where we corroborated responses from each agency, and found six discrepancies out of a total of 50 possibilities where an agency reported having a mechanism with another agency, but the other agency did not report that mechanism, which we considered reliable for our purposes. In order to increase the reliability of our data, we did not include these six discrepancies. Agency responses to our structured interviews were further evaluated by considering key practices for collaboration and key considerations for implementing interagency collaborative mechanisms.[7]

We conducted this performance audit from May 2013 to September 2014 in accordance with generally accepted government auditing standards. Those standards require that we plan and perform the audit to obtain sufficient, appropriate evidence to provide a reasonable basis for our findings and conclusions based on our audit objectives. We believe that the evidence obtained provides a reasonable basis for our findings and conclusions based on our audit objectives.

APPENDIX II: CHEMICAL INHALATION TOXICITY VALUES FOR SELECT AGENCIES

The following tables (tables 1-10) compare inhalation toxicity values for 10 selected chemicals developed by four federal agencies and one state agency: (1) the Agency for Toxic Substances and Disease Registry (ATSDR), (2) the Environmental Protection Agency (EPA), (3) the National Institute for Occupational Safety and Health (NIOSH), (4) the Occupational Safety and Health Administration (OSHA), and (5) California Environmental Protection Agency (CalEPA). Following are explanatory points provided by the agencies that are relevant, as noted, to some or all of the selected chemicals:

- **ATSDR.** To describe any differences in uses between its toxicity values and those of other selected agencies, ATSDR indicated that its Minimal Risk Levels (MRL) are screening levels for environmental exposures; OSHA and NIOSH values are for occupational exposure.
- **CalEPA.** To describe any differences in uses between its toxicity values and those of the other selected agencies, CalEPA reported that its Office of Environmental Health Hazard Assessment (OEHHA) is required to develop guidelines for conducting health risk assessments under the Air Toxics Hot Spots Program. Further, OEHHA developed

a Technical Support Document for derivation of reference exposure levels. The latest document addressing the derivation of noncancer reference exposure levels was adopted in December, 2008, and it describes acute, 8-hour, and chronic reference exposure levels. The document presents methodology that explicitly considers possible differential effects on the health of infants, children and other sensitive subpopulations and has been used to develop the reference exposure levels. Two additional Technical Support Documents have been developed, including one for cancer potency factors in May 2009, as well as a revised document for exposure assessment and stochastic analysis in October 2012. The Air Toxics Hot Spots Information and Assessment Act is designed to provide information to state and local agencies and to the general public on the extent of airborne emissions from stationary sources and their potential public health impacts. The act requires that the OEHHA develop risk assessment guidelines for the Air Toxics Hot Spots Program and the most recent guidance manual is available from August 2003. The guidance, intended to address health risks from airborne contaminants released by stationary sources, involves a methodology that is common to other regulatory risk assessment applications, particularly for California programs.

- **EPA.** To describe any differences in uses between its toxicity values and those of other selected agencies, EPA indicated that the agencies' values are developed in response to specific statutory requirements. EPA provided supplementary information about these requirements, as well as the purposes for the values developed by these agencies.
- **NIOSH.** To describe differences in uses between its toxicity values and those of other selected agencies, NIOSH indicated that its recommended exposure limits (REL) are developed for workplace exposures (other agencies develop values for environmental exposure); NIOSH RELs also support OSHA rulemaking.
- **OSHA.** For all chemicals except chromium VI, OSHA described the following differences in uses between its toxicity values and those of other selected agencies, and reasons why it developed its values: for most of its regulated chemicals, OSHA has not relied on an agency risk assessment to establish permissible exposure limits (PELs). Rather, these PELs were adopted shortly after formation of the agency in 1971 from approximately 400 occupational exposure limits that were based on the American Conference of Governmental Industrial

Hygienist's 1968 list of Threshold Value Limits. On January 19, 1989, OSHA published a final rule on air contaminants that lowered 212 of OSHA's existing PELs for toxic substances and set PELs for 164 toxic substances that had been previously unregulated. In doing so, OSHA relied heavily on the already published and widely accepted Threshold Limit Values published by the American Conference of Governmental Industrial Hygienists and the RELs developed by NIOSH. In 1992, a federal appellate court vacated these standards, holding that OSHA had failed to establish that the new standards were technologically and economically feasible.[1] As a result, OSHA resumed enforcing, and employers were required to comply with, the air contaminant exposure limits that were in effect prior to the issuance of the new limits on January 19, 1989. In reinstating the previous limits, OSHA said that it continued to believe that many these old limits were out of date (they predate 1968) and not sufficiently protective of employee health based on current scientific information and expert recommendations. In addition, OSHA observed that many of the substances for which OSHA had no PELs presented serious health hazards to employees. In commenting on the information in this appendix, OSHA officials stated that they continue to believe the limits contained in the 1989 rulemaking reduced significant risks of material impairment of health or functional capacity, and were technologically and economically feasible.

GAO note: the agencies listed below have developed toxicity values that vary in exposure. Specific terms included are "acute," which ATSDR defines as exposure of between 1 and 14 days, and which CalEPA defines as exposure of 1 hour. ATSDR defines "intermediate" exposure is being between 15 and 364 days. Both CalEPA and EPA define "chronic" exposure as being over the course of a lifetime, and ATSDR defines "chronic" as being exposure of 365 days or longer. NIOSH and OSHA develop toxicity values that with exposure levels that vary between exposure durations of 15 minutes, 8 hours, 10 hours, or a 40-hour week for a 45-year working lifetime. In addition, some agencies may use safety or uncertainty factors that protect susceptible populations. These factors may result in values that cannot be compared.

Table 1. Acrolein

	ATSDR	CalEPA	EPA	NIOSH	OSHA
Assessment date	2007	2008	2003	1988	1989
Number of reference values developed	2	3	1	2	2
First reference value (mg/m^3)	0.007 mg/m^3 (Acute: 1-14 days)	0.0025 mg/m^3 (Acute)	0.00002 mg/m^3 (Chronic)	0.25 mg/m^3 (10-hour TWA, 40-hours a week for a working lifetime)	0.25 mg/m^3 (8-hour TWA)
Second reference value (mg/m^3)	0.00009 mg/m^3(Intermediate 15-364 days)	0.00035 mg/m^3(Chronic)	-	0.8 mg/m^3(15-minute TWA STEL)	0.8 mg/m^3(15-minute STEL)
Third reference value (mg/m^3)	-	0.0007 mg/m^3(8-hour, general population)	-	-	-
Any differences in the values' uses	ATSDR's acute and intermediate MRLs for Acrolein are for up to 14 day exposure and 15-364 day exposure, respectively; CalEPA acute values are for 1-hour and 8-hour exposures. See introductory text.	See introductory text.	See introductory text.	NIOSH contributed to the OSHA assessment for acrolein as part of the 1988 OSHA PEL Update effort. NIOSH adopted the values as RELs.aSee introductory text.	See introductory text.

Legend:

ppm parts per million.

STEL short-term exposure limit.

Sources: Federal and state agency data. | GAO-14-763.

[a] The OSHA PEL for acrolein is 0.1 ppm (0.25 mg/m^3). This value was not changed in the1989 PEL Update final rule. The 0.3 ppm STEL was added in the PEL Update final rule, but was vacated by the 1992 court decision (see introductory text). Therefore, OSHA has the PEL but not a STEL for acrolein. NIOSH kept the limits developed in the 1988 effort.

Table 2. Carbon Disulfide

	ATSDR	CalEPA	EPA	NIOSH	OSHA
Assessment date	1996	1999 (acute), 2002 (chronic)	1995	1988	1989
Number of reference values developed	1	2	1	2	2
First reference value (mg/m^3)	0.9 mg/m^3 (Chronic: 365 days and longer)	6.2 mg/m^3 (Acute)	0.7 mg/m^3 (Chronic)	3 mg/m^3 (10-hour TWA, 40-hours a week for a working lifetime)	12 mg/m^3 (8-hour TWA)
Second reference value (mg/m^3)	-	0.8 mg/m^3 (Chronic)	-	30 mg/m^3 (15-minute TWA STEL)	36 mg/m^3 (STEL)
Any differences in the values' uses, additional notes	EPA used benchmark concentration for a point of departure of 6.3 ppm vs ATSDR LOAEL of 7.6 ppm; ATSDR used LOAEL of 7.6 and UF = 30. See introductory text.	See introductory text.	See introductory text.	NIOSH contributed to the OSHA assessment for carbon disulfide as part of the 1988 OSHA PEL Update effort. NIOSH had assessed carbon disulfide in a 1977 criteria document, and these limits were proposed in the 1988 PEL Update final rule. However, OSHA promulgated slightly higher limits because of feasibility concerns.aSee introductory text.	See introductory text.

LOAEL lowest-observed-adverse-effect level.

UF uncertainty factor.

Sources: Federal and state agency data. | GAO-14-763.

[a] The OSHA PEL is 20 ppm, 30 ppm ceiling and a 100 ppm 30-minute maximum peak. The 1989 PEL Update final rule established a 4 ppm TWA and 12 ppm STEL, plus a skin designation, but were vacated by the 1992 court decision (see introductory text). NIOSH kept the proposed limits developed in the 1988 effort of 1 ppm TWA and 10 ppm STEL.

Table 3. Chromium VI (Hexavalent Chromium)

	ATSDR	CalEPA	EPA	NIOSH	OSHA
Assessment date	2012	2001	1998	2013	2006
Number of reference values developed	3	1	2	1	1
First reference value (mg/m^3)	0.000005 mg/m^3 (aerosol mists) (Intermediate 15-364 days)	0.0002 mg/m^3 (except chromic trioxide) (Chronic)	0.000008 mg/m^3 (Chromic acid mists) (Chronic)	0.0002 mg/m^3(8-hour TWA, 40-hours a week for a working lifetime)	0.00025 mg/m^3 (1 x 10-3Risk Specific Exposure Level over 45-year working life)
Second reference value (mg/m^3)	0.000005 mg/m^3(aerosol mists) (Chronic > 364 days)	-	0.0001 mg/m^3(particulates) (Chronic)	-	-
Third reference value (mg/m^3)	0.0003 mg/m3(Particulates) (Intermediate 15-364 days)	-	-	-	-
Any differences in the values' uses, additional notes	EPA used a UF = 90, ATSDR used a UF = 100. CalEPA applied a UF = 300. See introductory text.	See introductory text.	See introductory text.	NIOSH develops Criteria Documents to synthesize and assess the health data supporting recommendations for controlling workplace exposures to hazardous substances, as directed in the Occupational Safety and Health Act.[a]See introductory text.	See introductory text.

Sources: Federal and state agency data. | GAO-14-763.

[a] NIOSH states that in 2013, NIOSH published Criteria for a Recommended Standard: Occupational Exposure to Hexavalent Chromium. This document presented the health basis for NIOSH's workplace recommendations and provides guidance for employers desiring to protect workers beyond what is required in the OSHA standard. Besides health effects, OSHA also considered, among other things, technological and economic feasibility when promulgating the Hexavalent Chromium Standard in 2006. The 2006 final rule establishes an 8-hour TWA exposure limit of 5 micrograms per cubic meter of air (5 μg/m^3). This is a reduction from the previous PEL of 52 μg/m^3. For chromium VI, OSHA indicated that the Risk Specific Exposure Level was the 8-hour, time-weighted average (TWA) projected to result in an excess lifetime cancer risk range of 5.2×10^{-4} to 2.3x10-3 over a 45-year working lifetime (i.e., ages 20 to 65). The estimate is based on a quantitative risk assessment used to support the OSHA 2006 occupational standard, which was developed pursuant to the requirements of the OSH Act. According to OSHA officials, the Risk Specific Exposure Level is not the enforceable OSHA PEL; the OSHA PEL was set at 5 μg/m^3, a level that was technologically and economically feasible in most Cr(VI) operations, most of the time. GAO note: OSHA issued the standard for chromium VI in February 2006. The 2006 final rule establishes an 8-hour TWA exposure limit of 5 micrograms per cubic meter of air (5 μg/m3), a reduction from the previous PEL of 52 μg/m^3.

Table 4. 1,4-Dioxane

	ATSDR	CalEPA	EPA	NIOSH	OSHA
Assessment date	2012	2008 (acute), 2000 (chronic)	2013	1988	1989
Number of reference values developed	3	2	1	2	1
First reference value (mg/m^3)	7.2 mg/m^3 (Acute: 1-14 days)	3 mg/m^3 (Acute)	0.03 mg/m^3 (Chronic)	Ca: "as low as feasible" (10-hour TWA, 40-hours a week for a working lifetime)	90 mg/m^3 (8-hour TWA)
Second reference value (mg/m^3)	0.72 mg/m^3 (Intermediate 15-364 days)	3 mg/m^3 (Chronic)	-	3.6 mg/m^3 (30-minute TWA ceiling value)	-

Table 4. (Continued)

	ATSDR	CalEPA	EPA	NIOSH	OSHA
Third reference value (mg/m^3)	0.11 mg/m^3 (Chronic > 364 days)	-	-	-	-
Any differences in the values' uses, additional notes.	EPA added an additional UF = 3 for database deficiency; ATSDR's acute and intermediate MRLs are for up to 14-day exposure and 15-364 day exposure, respectively; CalEPA acute values are for 1- hour and 8-hour exposures. ATSDR used a more recent 2009 study, Cal EPA used a 1974 study. See introductory text.	See introductory text.	See introductory text.	NIOSH contributed to the OSHA assessment for dioxane as part of the 1988 OSHA PEL Update effort. NIOSH had assessed dioxane in a 1977 criteria document and in 1988 continued to recommend a ceiling limit of 1 ppm and a (Ca) notation. OSHA adopted a 25 ppm PEL plus a skin notation in the 1988 PEL Update effort.[a] See introductory text.	See introductory text.

Legend:

Ca potential occupational carcinogen.

Sources: Federal and state agency data. | GAO-14-763.

[a] The OSHA PEL for dioxane is 100 ppm (360 mg/m^3) with a skin designation. These values were changed to 25 ppm plus a skin designation in the 1989 PEL Update final rule, but were later vacated by the 1992 court decision (see introductory text). NIOSH kept the REL it developed in the 1988 effort.

Table 5. Hydrogen Sulfide

	ATSDR	CalEPA	EPA	NIOSH	OSHA
Assessment date	2006	2008 (acute), 2000 (chronic)	2003	1988	1989
Number of reference values developed	2	2	1	1	2
First reference value (mg/m^3)	0.1 mg/m^3 (Acute: 1-14 days)	0.042 mg/m^3 (Acute)	0.002 mg/m^3 (Chronic)	15 mg/m^3 (10-minute TWA ceiling value)	15 mg/m^3 (8-hour TWA)
Second reference value (mg/m^3)	0.03 mg/m^3 (Intermediate 15-364 days)	0.01 mg/m^3 (Chronic)	-	-	21 mg/m^3 (15-minute STEL)
If aware of other values, any differences in the values' uses	EPA RfC used the same study as ATSDR intermediate MRL with additional UF for duration extrapolation. CalEPA chronic REL also used a subchronic study with additional UF for duration extrapolation. ATSDR acute MRL is for 1-14 days exposure; CalEPA acute REL is for 1-hour exposure. See introductory text.	See introductory text.	See introductory text.	NIOSH contributed to the OSHA assessment for hydrogen sulfide as part of the 1988 OSHA PEL Update effort. NIOSH had assessed hydrogen sulfide in a 1977 criteria document and the ceiling limit was recommended to OSHA in the 1988 PEL Update effort. OSHA chose limits of 10 ppm as an 8-hour TWA and 15 ppm as a STEL.[a] See introductory text.	See introductory text.

Legend:
RfC inhalation reference concentration.
Sources: Federal and state agency data. | GAO-14-763.
[a] The OSHA PEL for hydrogen sulfide is 20 ppm with a 50 ppm maximum peak (10-minute TWA). The exposure limits in the 1989 PEL Update final rule (10 ppm 8-hour TWA and 15 ppm STEL) were vacated by the 1992 court decision (see introductory text). NIOSH kept the limits it developed in the 1988 effort.

Table 6. Manganese

	ATSDR	**CalEPA**	**EPA**	**NIOSH**	**OSHA**
Assessment date	2012	2008	1993	1988	1989
Number of reference values developed	1	2	1	2	2
First reference value (mg/m^3)	0.0003 mg respirable manganese/m^3 (Chronic: 365 days and longer)	0.00017 mg/m^3 (8-hour, general population)	0.00005 mg/m^3 (Chronic)	1 mg/m^3 (10-hour TWA, 40-hours a week for a working lifetime)	1 mg/m^3 (8-hour TWA)
Second reference value (mg/m^3)	-	0.00009 mg/m^3 (Chronic)	-	3 mg/m^3 (15-minute TWA STEL)	3 mg/m^3 (15-minute STEL)
Any differences in the values' uses, additional notes	ATSDR chronic MRL used BMC10, EPA chronic RfC used LOAEL, CalEPA chronic REL used BMCL05, all three based on Roels et al. 1992. See introductory text.	See introductory text.	See introductory text.	NIOSH contributed to the OSHA assessment for manganese as part of the 1988 OSHA PEL Update effort.[a] See introductory text.	See introductory text.

Legend:

BMC Benchmark Concentration.

BMCL Benchmark Concentration Confidence Limit.

Sources: Federal and state agency data. | GAO-14-763.

[a] The OSHA PEL for manganese is a ceiling value of 5 mg/m^3. This was changed in the 1989 PEL Update final rule to an 8-hour TWA of 1 mg/m^3 and a STEL of 3 mg/m^3, but were vacated by the 1992 court decision (see introductory text). NIOSH kept the limits developed in the 1988 effort.

Table 7. Mercury

	ATSDR	CalEPA	EPA	NIOSH	OSHA
Assessment date	1999	2008	1995	1988	1989
Number of reference values developed	1	3	1	1	4
First reference value (mg/m3)	0.0002 mg/m^3 Chronic: 365 days and longer)	0.0006 mg/m^3 (Acute)	0.0003 mg/m^3 (Chronic)	0.05 mg/m^3 (10-hour TWA, 40-hours a week for a working lifetime)	0.005 mg/m^3 (vapor) (8-hour TWA)
Second reference value (mg/m3)	-	0.00006 mg/m^3 (8-hour, general population)	-	-	0.01 mg/m^3 (organo) (8-hour TWA)
Third reference value (mg/m^3)	-	0.00003 mg/m^3 (Chronic)	-	-	0.03 mg/m^3 (organo) (15-minute STEL)
Fourth reference value (mg/m3)	-	-	-	-	0.01 mg/m^3 (aryl and inorganic) (Ceiling - not to exceed at any time)

Table 7. (Continued)

	ATSDR	CalEPA	EPA	NIOSH	OSHA
Any differences in the values' uses, additional notes	EPA used UF = 30; CalEPA used UF = 300; ATSDR used UF = 30. EPA and CalEPA used multiple studies to identify a LOAEL of 0.025 vs ATSDR using 0.026 from Fawer et al. EPA and CalEPA adjusted for ventilation rates. See introductory text.	See introductory text.	See introductory text.	NIOSH contributed to the OSHA assessment for mercury as part of the 1988 OSHA PEL Update effort. NIOSH had assessed mercury in a 1973 criteria document and the REL of 0.05 mg/m3was proposed to OSHA as part of that process.[a] See introductory text.	See introductory text.

Sources: Federal and state agency data. | GAO-14-763.

[a] The OSHA PEL for mercury is a ceiling value of 0.1 mg/m^3. This was changed in the 1989 PEL Update final rule to an 8-hour TWA of 0.05 mg/m^3, but was vacated by the 1992 court decision (see introductory text). NIOSH kept the limits developed in the 1988 effort.

Table 8. Styrene

	ATSDR	CalEPA	EPA	NIOSH	OSHA
Assessment date	2010	2008 (acute), 2000 (chronic)	1992	1988	1989
Number of reference values developed	2	2	1	2	2
First reference value (mg/m^3)	21 mg/m^3(Acute: 1-14 days)	21 mg/m^3 (Acute)	1 mg/m^3 (Chronic)	215 mg/m^3 (10-hour TWA, 40-hours a week for a working lifetime)	215 mg/m^3 (8-hour TWA)
Second reference value (mg/m3)	0.84 mg/m^3 (Chronic: 365 days or longer)	0.9 mg/m^3 (Chronic)	-	425 mg/m^3 (15-minute TWA STEL)	425 mg/m^3 (15-minute STEL)
Any differences in the values' uses, additional notes	Chronic inhalation MRL used a more recent study (Benignus et al 2005). Acute MRL is for 1-14 days exposure, CalEPA acute REL is for 1-hour exposure. See introductory text.	See introductory text.	See introductory text.	NIOSH contributed to the OSHA assessment for styrene as part of the 1988 OSHA PEL Update effort. NIOSH had assessed styrene in a 1983 criteria document and the REL of 50 ppm/STEL of 100 ppm was recommended to OSHA in the PEL Update final rule. OSHA agreed.[a] See introductory text.	See introductory text.

Sources: Federal and state agency data. | GAO-14-763.

[a] The OSHA PEL for styrene is 100 ppm as an 8-hour TWA with a ceiling limit of 200 ppm with a 600 ppm 5-minute maximum peak in any 3-hours. This was changed in the 1989 PEL Update final rule to a 50 ppm 8-hour TWA and 100 ppm 15-minute STEL, but were vacated by the 1992 court decision (see introductory text). NIOSH kept the limits developed in the 1988 effort.

Table 9. Toluene

	ATSDR	CalEPA	EPA	NIOSH	OSHA
Assessment date	2000	2008 (acute) 2000 (chronic)	2005	1988	1989
Number of reference values developed	2	2	1	2	2
First reference value (mg/m^3)	3.8 mg/m^3 (Acute: 1-14 days)	37 mg/m^3 (Acute)	5 mg/m^3 (Chronic)	375 mg/m^3 (8-hour TWA, 40-hours a week for a working lifetime)	375 mg/m^3 (8-hour TWA)
Second reference value (mg/m^3)	0.3 mg/m^3 (Chronic: 365 days and longer)	0.3 mg/m^3 (Chronic)	-	560 mg/m^3 (15-minute TWA STEL)	560 mg/m^3 (15-minute STEL)
Any differences in the values' uses, additional notes	EPA's RfC is based on an arithmetic mean of NOAEL values from 10 different studies that was chosen to represent an average point of departure. See introductory text.	See introductory text.	See introductory text.	NIOSH contributed to the OSHA assessment for toluene as part of the 1988 OSHA PEL Update effort. NIOSH had assessed toluene in a 1973 criteria document but the reassessment lowered the REL. OSHA adopted the 100 ppm PEL in the PEL Update final rule.[a] See introductory text.	See introductory text.

Legend:
NOAEL No-observed-adverse-effect level.
Sources: Federal and state agency data. | GAO-14-763.

[a] The OSHA PEL for toluene is 200 ppm as an 8-hour TWA with a ceiling limit of 300 ppm and a 10-minute maximum peak of 500 ppm. This was changed in the 1989 PEL Update final rule to a 100 ppm 8-hour TWA and a 150 ppm STEL, but were vacated by the 1992 court decision (see introductory text). NIOSH kept the limits developed in the 1988 effort.

Table 10. Trichloroethylene (TCE)

	ATSDR	CalEPA	EPA	NIOSH	OSHA
Assessment date	2013	2000	2011	1988	1989
Number of reference values developed	1	1	1	2	2
First reference value (mg/m^3)	0.002 mg/m^3 (Chronic: 365 days and longer)	0.6 mg/m^3 (Chronic)	0.002 mg/m^3 (Chronic)	134 mg/m^3 (10-hour TWA, 40-hours a week for a working lifetime (all uses except as an anesthetic agent). Also noted as a carcinogen.	270 mg/m^3 (8-hour TWA)
Second reference value (mg/m^3)	-	-	-	10.7 mg/m^3 (60-minute ceiling during the use of TCE as an anesthetic agent)	1080 mg/m^3 (15-minute STEL)
Any differences in the values' uses, additional note	ATSDR adopted EPA's RfC value. Cal EPA based on a LOAEL of 11.4 ppm in Vandervort and Polnkoff (1973). See introductory text.	See introductory text.	See introductory text.	NIOSH contributed to the OSHA assessment for trichloroethylene as part of the 1988 OSHA PEL Update effort. NIOSH had assessed trichloroethylene in a 1978 criteria document and the REL of 25 ppm proposed in the PEL Update. However, OSHA promulgated a PEL of 50 ppm in the 1989 final rule.[a] See introductory text.	See introductory text.

Sources: Federal and state agency data. | GAO-14-763.

[a] The OSHA PEL for trichloroethylene is 100 ppm as an 8-hour TWA with a ceiling limit of 200 ppm and a 300 ppm 5-minute maximum peak in any 2 hours. This was changed in the 1989 PEL Update final rule to a 50 ppm TWA and a 100 ppm STEL, but were vacated by the 1992 court decision (see introductory text). NIOSH kept the limits from the 1978 criteria document. OSHA values in the 1989 final rule were 50 ppm TWA and 200 ppm STEL and the NIOSH values are 25 ppm TWA and 2 ppm ceiling only during use as an anesthetic agent.

End Notes

[1] Agencies use the term "chemicals" and "substances" synonymously. For the purposes of this report, we will use the term chemicals.

[2] Agencies also assess chemicals' risk to the environment; however, these assessments are outside the scope of this review.

[3] These four components are outlined in the 1983 National Academies' National Research Council, *Risk Assessment in the Federal Government: Managing the Process* (commonly known as the Red Book). Hazard identification examines whether a stressor, or chemical, has the potential to cause harm to humans and/or ecological systems, and if so, under what circumstances. Dose-response assessment examines the numerical relationship between exposure and effects. Exposure assessment examines what is known about the frequency, timing, and levels of human contact with a stressor. A risk characterization conveys the risk assessor's judgment as to the nature and presence or absence of risks, along with information about how the risk was assessed, where assumptions and uncertainties still exist, and where policy choices will need to be made.

[4] Toxicity represents the degree to which a chemical is harmful. In this report, the terms toxicity and hazard are used synonymously.

[5] Other federal agencies perform chemical toxicity assessment activities but we limited our review to the key agencies that, as part of their primary mission, perform assessments of chemicals to which there is exposure in the environment, as opposed to exposure from chemicals in or on specific consumer products.

[6] GAO, *Additional Opportunities to Reduce Fragmentation, Overlap, and Duplication and Achieve Other Financial Benefits*, GAO-14-343SP (Washington, D.C.: Apr. 8, 2014). GAO is required to conduct routine investigations to identify programs, agencies, offices, and initiatives with duplicative goals and activities within departments and governmentwide and report annually to Congress in accordance with Section 21 of Pub. L. No. 111-139 (2010).

[7] GAO, *High-Risk Series: An Update,* GAO-09-271 (Washington, D.C.: Jan. 22, 2009).

[8] GAO, *Chemical Assessments: Low Productivity and New Interagency Review Process Limit the Usefulness and Credibility of EPA's Integrated Risk Information System*, GAO-08-440 (Washington, D.C.: Mar. 7, 2008).

[9] GAO, *Chemical Assessments: Challenges Remain with EPA's Integrated Risk Information System Program,* GAO-12-42 (Washington, D.C.: Dec. 9, 2011).

[10] GAO, *High-Risk Series: An Update,* GAO-13-283 (Washington, D.C.: Feb. 14, 2013).

[11] We selected the following 12 state agencies: Alaska Department of Environmental Conservation, the Arizona Department of Health Services, the California Environmental Protection Agency, the Delaware Department of Health and Social Services, the Delaware Department of Natural Resources and Environmental Control, the Minnesota Department of Health, the Minnesota Pollution Control Agency, the Missouri Department of Health & Senior Services, the New Jersey Department of Environmental Protection, the New York Department of Environmental Conservation, the Oklahoma Department of Environmental Quality, and the Texas Commission on Environmental Quality. We interviewed officials from two agencies within Minnesota and Delaware because state officials from these two states indicated that chemical toxicity assessment responsibilities were split among different state agencies, and they recommended that we interview those other agency officials. Because this was a nonprobability sample, the information and perspectives that we obtained from these state agencies are not generalizable to other state agencies.

[12] We did not include NTP among the selected federal agencies because it does not develop quantitative toxicity values and included CalEPA to provide an illustrative example of a state's toxicity values.

[13] We have previously reported that GAO uses the term "collaboration" broadly to include interagency activities that others have variously defined as "cooperation," "coordination," "integration," or "networking." GAO has done so since there are no commonly accepted definitions for these terms, and we are unable to make definitive distinctions between these different types of interagency activities. Although there is no commonly accepted definition for collaboration, we define it as any joint activity by two or more organizations that is intended to produce more public value than could be produced when the organizations act alone. See GAO, *Results-Oriented Government: Practices That Can Help Enhance and Sustain Collaboration among Federal Agencies*, GAO-06-15 (Washington, D.C.: Oct. 21, 2005).

[14] See GAO-06-15; GAO, *Managing for Results: Implementation Approaches Used to Enhance Collaboration in Interagency Groups*, GAO-14-220 (Washington, D.C.: Feb. 14, 2014) and *Managing for Results: Key Considerations for Implementing Interagency Collaborative Mechanisms*, GAO-12-1022 (Washington, D.C.: Sept. 27, 2012).

[15] See Pub. L. No. 96-510 (1980), *codified as amended at* 42 U.S.C. §§ 9601-9675. CERCLA, also known as Superfund, provides broad federal authority to respond directly to releases or threatened releases of hazardous substances that may endanger public health or the environment.

[16] The National Priorities List (NPL) is the list of national priorities among the known releases or threatened releases of hazardous substances, pollutants, or contaminants throughout the United States and its territories. According to EPA, the NPL is intended primarily to guide EPA in determining which sites warrant further investigation and identifying what cleanup actions might be appropriate. See 42 U.S.C. § 9605(a)(8). Currently, the NPL includes 1,320 sites, and another 51 sites have been proposed.

[17] CERCLA requires toxicological profiles to include, at a minimum, (a) an examination, summary, and interpretation of available toxicological information and epidemiologic evaluations on a hazardous substance in order to ascertain the levels of significant human exposure for the substance and the associated acute, subacute, and chronic health effects; (b) a determination of whether adequate information on the health effects of each substance is available or in the process of development to determine levels of exposure which present a significant risk to human health of acute, subacute, and chronic health effects; and (c) where appropriate, an identification of toxicological testing needed to identify the types or levels of exposure that may present significant risk of adverse health effects in humans. 42 U.S.C. § 9604(i)(3)(A)-(C).

[18] 15 U.S.C § 2601 et. seq. In 1976, Congress passed TSCA to provide EPA with the authority to obtain more information on chemicals and to regulate those chemicals that EPA determines pose unreasonable risks to human health or the environment.

[19] 42 U.S.C. § 300f et. seq. Under the Safe Drinking Water Act, EPA is authorized to regulate contaminants in public drinking water systems.

[20] 42 U.S.C. § 7401 et. seq. The Clean Air Act is a comprehensive federal law that regulates air pollution from stationary and mobile sources.

[21] 42 U.S.C. §§6901 et. seq. (2012). The Resource Conservation and Recovery Act requires, among other things, companies that treat, store, or dispose of hazardous waste to obtain a permit specifying how their facilities will safely manage that waste.

[22] 33 U.S.C. § 1251 et. seq. The 1972 Clean Water Act aimed to "restore and maintain the chemical, physical, and biological integrity of the nation's waters."

[23] 7 U.S.C § 136 et. seq. The Federal Insecticide, Fungicide, and Rodenticide Act, as amended, generally requires registration of pesticides and authorizes EPA to limit the distribution and sale of unregistered pesticides to the extent necessary to prevent unreasonable adverse effects on the environment.

[24] Although EPA officials indicated that the Office of the Science Advisor does not conduct its own toxicity assessments, EPA officials told us it provides leadership and facilitates the integration of the highest quality science and technology policy into the agency's policies and decisions. According to these officials, the Science Advisor chairs the Science and Technology Policy Council, which may approve actions taken by the agency's Risk Assessment Forum, a standing committee of senior EPA scientists established to promote agency-wide consensus on difficult and controversial risk assessment issues and to ensure that this consensus is incorporated into appropriate agency risk assessment guidance.

[25] ORD also develops Integrated Science Assessments, which are used by EPA's Office of Air and Radiation to develop ambient air quality standards for the Criteria Air Pollutants under the Clean Air Act.

[26] Under its IRIS Program, EPA (1) identifies a chemical's toxicity, or hazardous properties, which are the potential noncancer and cancer human health effects of exposure to a chemical, and (2) assesses the dose-response relationship between exposure to a chemical and the resultant health effects, which describes the magnitude of hazard for potential noncancer effects and increased cancer risk. A human health risk assessment characterizes the nature and magnitude of health risks to humans from exposure to chemical contaminants that may be present in the environment. IRIS toxicity assessments are used along with other information to prepare human health risk assessments. A typical IRIS toxicity assessment contains a qualitative hazard identification and quantitative dose-response assessment.

[27] See, for example, GAO, *Toxic Substances: EPA Has Increased Efforts to Assess and Control Chemicals but Could Strengthen Its Approach*, GAO-13-249 (Washington, D.C.: Mar. 22, 2013).

[28] See, for example, GAO-13-249.

[29] This use is consistent with the fact that media-specific environmental laws, such as the Clean Air Act and Clean Water Act, are available to limit the concentration of contaminants in water or the ambient air, and TSCA generally requires EPA to defer action to such other laws. However, information on such continuous exposures is still critical for regulation under TSCA. For example, to promulgate a rule under section 6 of TSCA, EPA must establish the effects of a chemical on health and the environment and the magnitude of the exposure of human beings and the environment to such a chemical. See GAO-13-249.

[30] Region 2 serves New Jersey, New York, Puerto Rico, the U.S. Virgin Islands, and eight Tribal Nations.

[31] Region 9 serves Arizona, California, Hawaii, and Nevada, as well as a number of Tribal Nations and Pacific Island locations.

[32] 42 U.S.C § 241(b)(4).

[33] NIEHS established OHAT to serve as an environmental health resource to the public and to regulatory and health agencies.

[34] NTP's activities for this program–formally called Toxicology Testing in the 21st Century, or Tox21 for short, are in relation to an MOU between EPA, the Food and Drug Administration, the National Institutes of Health, and the NTP.

[35] 29 U.S.C. § 651 et. seq.

[36] 29 U.S.C. § 655(b)(5).

[37] See, e.g., 79 Fed. Reg. 20316, 20561(2104).

[38] According to OSHA data, hexavalent chromium is usually produced by an industrial process and is known to cause cancer. In addition, it targets the respiratory system, kidneys, liver, skin, and eyes. Chromium metal is added to alloy steel and may be used as pigments in dyes, paints, inks, and plastics. It also may be used as an anticorrosive agent added to paints, primers, and other surface coatings. Crystalline silica is a very small particle that is created during work operations involving stone, rock, concrete, brick, block, mortar, and industrial sand that, when inhaled, puts workers at risk for silicosis, lung cancer, chronic obstructive pulmonary disease, and kidney disease. Beryllium is a brittle, steel-gray metal found as a component of coal, oil, certain rock minerals, volcanic dust, and soil. Elemental beryllium is the second lightest of all metals and is used in a wide variety of applications.

[39] These analyses are necessary because the Supreme Court has held that the OSH Act requires that standards be both technologically and economically feasible. *Am. Textile Mfrs. Inst. v. Donovan*, 452 U.S. 490, 513 n.31 (1981).

[40] 29 U.S.C. § 651 et. seq. NIOSH also recommends standards to the Mine Safety and Health Administration under the Federal Mine Safety and Health Act of 1977. See 30 U.S.C. § 811(a)(1).

[41] See 29 U.S.C. § 671.

[42] See 29 U.S.C. 669(a)(3).

[43] The NIOSH Pocket Guide to Chemical Hazards is intended as a source of general industrial hygiene information on several hundred chemicals for workers, employers, and occupational health professionals.

[44] Unlike OSHA standards, NIOSH recommendations are not binding on employers. E.g., Bergfeld v. Unimin Corp., 226 F.Supp.2d 970, 975 (N.D. Iowa 2002).

[45] According to EPA, MTBE was used as a fuel additive in motor gasoline. It is one of a group of chemicals commonly known as “oxygenates” because they raise the oxygen content of gasoline. At room temperature, MTBE is a volatile, flammable and colorless liquid that dissolves rather easily in water.

[46] GAO-14-343SP.

[47] GAO, *Opportunities to Reduce Potential Duplication in Government Programs, Save Tax Dollars, and Enhance Revenue*, GAO-11-318SP (Washington, D.C.: Mar. 1, 2011).

[48] ATSDR developed three toxicity values for 1,4-dioxane at varying exposure durations: (1) acute defined as being 1 to 14 days; (2) intermediate, defined as being 15 to 364 days; and (3) chronic, defined as being greater than 364 days. OSHA’s value is for an 8-hour occupational exposure.

[49] GAO-11-318SP.

[50] GAO-11-318SP.

[51] GAO-14-343SP.

[52] According to EPA officials, EPA IRIS values typically are concerned with chronic (lifetime) exposures, but EPA Program Offices (e.g., OCSPP, OW, OSWER, and OAR) consider other durations of exposure when assessing risk.

[53] According to EPA’s website, hexavalent chromium occurs naturally in the environment from the erosion of natural chromium deposits, and it can also be produced by industrial processes.

[54] We previously reported in May 2013 that the IRIS Program solicits chemical nominations from stakeholders, such as EPA offices, other federal agencies, and the public. In their nomination forms, stakeholders send EPA the names of chemicals and the reasons for

requesting that IRIS toxicity assessments be developed or updated, among other information.

[55] The different mechanisms by which agencies coordinate do not necessarily indicate better quality or more effective coordination. Whether the type of coordination mechanism affected quality of effectiveness is beyond the scope of this review. For a discussion of mechanisms for interagency collaboration and definitions, see Figure 1 in GAO-12-1022.

[56] According to an OSHA fact sheet, Nanotechnology is "the understanding and control of matter at the nanoscale, at dimensions between approximately 1 and 100 nanometers (nm)." Nanomaterials can be used in novel applications, such as making stain-free textiles or targeting drugs selectively to cancerous cells. Nanotechnology has the potential to impact many industries, including electronics, healthcare, construction and consumer products. For recent GAO reports on nanotechnology, see GAO, *Nanomanufacturing: Emergence and Implications for U.S. Competitiveness, the Environment, and Human Health*, GAO-14-181SP (Washington, D.C.: Jan. 31, 2014) and GAO, *Nanotechnology: Improved Performance Information Needed for Environmental, Health, and Safety Research*, GAO-12-427 (Washington, D.C.: May 21, 2012).

[57] Officials from 4 out of the 10 states we reviewed—California, Minnesota, New Jersey, and Texas—responded that their states have developed their own chemical toxicity assessment information in the last 5 years; officials from the remaining 6 out of the 10 states we reviewed—Alaska, Arizona, Delaware, Missouri, New York, and Oklahoma— responded that their states have not developed their own assessment information in the last 5 years and relied exclusively on the federal government for toxicity assessment information.

[58] GAO-13-249.

[59] In 2005, we suggested that Congress consider authorizing EPA to share with other entities information chemical companies submit to EPA and identify as CBI, subject to regulations to be established by EPA in consultation with the chemical industry and other interested parties. See GAO, *Chemical Regulation: Options Exist to Improve EPA's Ability to Assess Health Risks and Manage Its Chemical Review Program*, GAO-05-458 (Washington, D.C.: June 13, 2005). We recommended that the EPA Administrator should revise the agency's regulations to require that companies reassert claims of confidentiality submitted to EPA under TSCA within a certain time period after the information is initially claimed as confidential. EPA responded by exploring ways to reduce the number of inappropriate and over-broad claims of confidentiality by companies that submit data to EPA. In March 2013, we found that EPA established new policies in 2011 requiring chemical companies to substantiate claims that information they provide is CBI, which, according to EPA officials, significantly decreased CBI claims for those data. Also in March 2013, we found that EPA does not have a strategy for how the agency will meet the challenge of obtaining the toxicity and exposure data it will need for conducting risk assessments for all 83 chemicals in its work plan under its existing TSCA authority. Specifically, we found that EPA has not broadly sought toxicity and exposure data that companies submit to the European Chemicals Agency or exposure-related data from chemical processors and instead plans to obtain these data, as needed, on a case-bycase basis from chemical companies. However, the agency's strategy does not discuss how EPA would execute these plans or how the data obtained would be used to inform its ongoing or future risk assessment activities, if at all. See GAO-13-249.

[60] The provisions for disclosure of chemical data in section 14 of TSCA specify when EPA may disclose chemical information it obtains under the act. Chemical companies can claim certain information, such as data disclosing chemical processes, as confidential business

information. EPA generally must protect confidential business information (CBI) against public disclosure unless necessary to protect against an unreasonable risk of injury to health or the environment. Other federal agencies and federal contractors can obtain access to this CBI in order to carry out their responsibilities. EPA may also disclose certain data from health and safety studies.

[61] GAO, *Live Animal Imports: Agencies Need Better Collaboration to Reduce the Risk of Animal-Related Diseases*, GAO-11-9 (Washington, D.C.: Nov. 8, 2010). See also GAO-12-1022.

[62] GAO-12-1022. To identify mechanisms that the federal government uses to lead and implement interagency collaboration, we conducted a literature review of academic work, interviewed a number of experts in governmental collaboration, and analyzed a sample of our prior work. See GAO-12-1022 for additional details on the methodology for identifying these mechanisms.

[63] Congress established OSTP in 1976 to advise the President and others within the Executive Office of the President on considerations of science and technology in federal policy, plans, and programs. OSTP is also charged with leading interagency efforts to develop and implement sound science and technology policies, among other things.

[64] GAO-12-427.

[65] GAO, *Environmental Health: Action Needed to Sustain Agencies' Collaboration on Pharmaceuticals in Drinking Water*, GAO-11-346 (Washington, D.C.: Aug. 8, 2011).

End Notes for Appendix I

[1] Other federal agencies perform chemical toxicity assessment activities, but we limited our review to the key agencies that, as part of their primary mission, perform assessments of chemicals to which there is exposure in the environment, as opposed to exposure from chemicals in or on specific consumer products.

[2] We selected the following 12 state agencies with the assistance of an Interstate Technology & Regulatory Council (ITRC) official, who is knowledgeable in state chemical toxicity assessment activities: the Alaska Department of Environmental Conservation, the Arizona Department of Health Services, the California Environmental Protection Agency, the Delaware Department of Health and Social Services, the Delaware Department of Natural Resources and Environmental Control, the Minnesota Department of Health, the Minnesota Pollution Control Agency, the Missouri Department of Health & Senior Services, the New Jersey Department of Environmental Protection, the New York Department of Environmental Conservation, the Oklahoma Department of Environmental Quality, and the Texas Commission on Environmental Quality.

[3] Established in 1995, ITRC is a state-led, national coalition of personnel from the environmental regulatory agencies of all 50 states and the District of Columbia, three federal agencies, tribes, and public and industry stakeholders. The organization is devoted to reducing barriers to, and speeding interstate deployment of, better, more cost-effective, innovative environmental techniques. ITRC operates as a committee of the Environmental Research Institute of the States, a Section 501(c)(3) public charity that supports the Environmental Council of the States through its educational and research activities aimed at improving the environment in the United States and providing a forum for state environmental policymakers.

[4] We selected the following 10 chemicals: (1) acrolein, (2) carbon disulfide, (3) chromium VI (hexavalent chromium), (4) 1,4-dioxane, (5) hydrogen sulfide, (6) manganese, (7) mercury, (8) styrene, (9) toluene, and (10) trichloroethylene (TCE).

[5] We spoke with the following six EPA program and regional offices: (1) Office of Pesticide Programs; (2) Office of Pollution Prevention and Toxics; (3) Office of Research and Development; (4) Office of Water; (5) Region 2, which serves New Jersey, New York, Puerto Rico, U.S. Virgin Islands, and eight Tribal Nations; and (6) Region 9, which serves Arizona, California, Hawaii, Nevada, Pacific Islands, and 148 Tribal Nations.

[6] We have previously reported that GAO uses the term "collaboration" broadly to include interagency activities that others have variously defined as "cooperation," "coordination," "integration," or "networking." GAO has done so since there are no commonly accepted definitions for these terms, and we are unable to make definitive distinctions between these different types of interagency activities. Although there is no commonly accepted definition for collaboration, we define it as any joint activity by two or more organizations that is intended to produce more public value than could be produced when the organizations act alone. See GAO, *Results-Oriented Government: Practices That Can Help Enhance and Sustain Collaboration among Federal Agencies*, GAO-06-15 (Washington, D.C.: Oct. 21, 2005).

[7] See GAO-06-15; GAO-14-220; and GAO-12-1022.

End Note for Appendix II

[1] American Federation of Labor and Congress of Industrial Organizations v. Occupational Safety and Health Administration, 965 F.2d 962 (11th Cir. 1992).

In: Chemical Risk Assessment Activities … ISBN: 978-1-63485-058-2
Editor: Naomi Sutton

Chapter 2

CHEMICALS MANAGEMENT: OBSERVATIONS ON HUMAN HEALTH RISK ASSESSMENT AND MANAGEMENT BY SELECTED FOREIGN PROGRAMS*

U.S. Government Accountability Office

The Honorable Edward Markey
Ranking Member
Subcommittee on Superfund, Waste Management,
nd Regulatory Oversight
Committee on Environment and Public Works
United States Senate

Dear Senator Markey:

To manage the thousands of chemicals in commercial use, decision makers around the world rely on information derived from assessments that examine the risks these substances may pose to human health and the environment. The Environmental Protection Agency's (EPA) Integrated Risk Information System (IRIS) Program and others conduct such assessments. EPA's assessments provide a foundation for the agency's risk management decisions, such as whether to establish air and water quality standards to

* This is an edited, reformatted and augmented version of The United States Government Accountability Office publication, GAO-16-111R, dated October 9, 2015.

protect the public from exposure to particular toxic chemicals. Consequently, risk assessments are a critical component of EPA's capacity to support scientifically sound environmental decisions, policies, and regulations under a variety of statutes. Various foreign programs, such as Canada's Chemicals Management Plan (CMP), Australia's Inventory Multi-tiered Assessment and Prioritisation (IMAP) framework, and the World Health Organization's (WHO)[1] International Agency for Research on Cancer (IARC) Monographs Programme and International Programme on Chemical Safety (IPCS) also conduct risk assessments or components of risk assessments.[2] In addition, foreign programs and foreign countries, including Canada, take risk management actions to prevent and reduce threats posed by chemicals to human health and the environment.

We have repeatedly reported that EPA's ability to fulfill its mission of protecting public health and the environment is critically dependent on credible and timely assessments of the risks posed by chemicals.[3] In January 2009, we added transforming EPA's processes for assessing and controlling toxic chemicals to the list of government operations that are high risk[4] based on our reports on EPA's IRIS Program and EPA's work under the Toxic Substances Control Act (TSCA).[5] Regarding the IRIS Program, we previously identified long-standing challenges in such areas as developing sufficient assessment information, and determining the program's need for people and resources. For example, as we reported in February 2015, after more than 2 years, EPA is still developing an action plan to address these capacity issues.[6] EPA has, however, made some progress in this area by continuing to monitor the IRIS Program and to implement our December 2011 recommendation to submit assessments for independent review to an entity with scientific and technical credibility. For example, EPA presented a plan for implementing the National Academies' suggestions for improving IRIS assessments, as stated in its "Roadmap for Revision" report.[7] In addition, EPA told us about its ongoing work to develop a new screening-level assessment product.[8] Regarding TSCA, EPA is authorized to obtain information on the risks of chemicals and to control those the agency determines pose an unreasonable risk.[9] As we also reported in June 2005 and February 2015, EPA has found much of TSCA difficult to implement, and the agency faced challenges to banning or placing limits on the production or use of chemicals due to a legal threshold that EPA has found difficult to meet.[10] Consequently, EPA has used its authority to limit or ban the use of only five existing chemicals or chemical classes since TSCA was enacted in 1976.[11]

In recent years, congressional committees have held a number of hearings and considered potential bills to reform TSCA.[12] In our February 2015 High-Risk Series report, we reported that EPA's Administrator and top management have demonstrated a strong leadership commitment by publicly stating their focus to improve the IRIS Program and implement TSCA as it currently exists.[13] In addition, the agency has publicly committed to responding to our recommendations, utilizing TSCA to the fullest extent of the law, and assisting congressional committees as they work to revise the 1976 law.

Given EPA's interest in addressing these long-standing problems and concern among lawmakers about how chemicals are assessed and managed, we gathered information about methods used by selected foreign programs. While each program operates within a different institutional structure, the descriptions in this report may offer perspectives that EPA and the Congress may find useful when considering improvements to the IRIS Program, TSCA, or other chemicals management efforts at EPA. We performed our work under the authority of the Comptroller General to assist Congress with its oversight responsibilities. This report examines: (1) how selected foreign programs conduct risk assessment activities to understand the human health risks of certain chemicals and (2) how Canada manages the human health risks of chemicals identified as toxic under the *Canadian Environmental Protection Act, 1999* (CEPA 1999).[14]

To address these objectives, we took several steps. To determine how selected foreign programs conduct risk assessment activities to understand the human health risks of certain chemicals, we asked EPA officials and academics with relevant expertise for their views on which programs produce quality chemical assessments that we might consider for our study. From those, we selected four for further review: Canada's CMP, Australia's IMAP framework, and WHO's IARC Monographs Programme and IPCS. Due to ongoing trade negotiations between the United States and the European Union that address, among other things, coordination of chemical regulatory regimes, we did not include European Union programs in our review. We met with representatives from each of the four programs we selected and reviewed numerous documents with information on relevant laws, policies, and risk assessments. We also interviewed stakeholders representing three industry and three environmental groups—identified by consulting our prior work and by soliciting input from EPA officials and academics with relevant knowledge—to understand their views on selected programs' processes. Their views cannot be generalized to the population of these groups but provided valuable insights. To determine how Canada manages the human health risks of chemicals identified as toxic under CEPA 1999, we met with relevant officials from Canada and reviewed documentation provided by those officials and published on their website. We focused on the Canadian approach under CEPA 1999 because it is regularly discussed in the debate on reforming TSCA and because Environment Canada and Health Canada are the only programs in our study that also conduct risk management activities. Enclosure I provides a more detailed presentation of our objectives, scope, and methodology.

We conducted this performance audit from March 2014 to October 2015 in accordance with generally accepted government auditing standards. Those standards require that we plan and perform the audit to obtain sufficient, appropriate evidence to provide a reasonable basis for our findings and conclusions based on our audit objectives. We believe that the evidence obtained provides a reasonable basis for our findings and conclusions based on our audit objectives.

RESULTS IN BRIEF

The foreign programs we reviewed—Canada's CMP, Australia's IMAP framework, and WHO's IARC Monographs Programme and IPCS—assess the human health risks of chemicals using similar analytic approaches, such as using specific criteria to determine which assessments to prioritize. However, there are some key differences in what the programs emphasize in their assessments. Canada and Australia's programs emphasize the use of screening assessments[15]—assessments that vary in complexity ranging from a rapid screen of information to using more complex approaches, depending on what officials determine is needed to adequately understand the risks of each chemical or other substance[16]—and WHO's IARC Monographs Programme and IPCS emphasize review by international experts.

Canada has used various measures to manage the human health risks of toxic chemicals under CEPA 1999. Specifically, according to Canada's guide to CEPA 1999 and Canadian officials, for chemicals and other substances determined to be toxic under CEPA 1999 and proposed for addition to CEPA 1999's List of Toxic Substances,[17] Canada may use a variety of mechanisms to manage identified human health risks, such as regulations, pollution prevention plan notices, and Significant New Activity provisions.

BACKGROUND

Tens of thousands of chemicals are listed for commercial use with federal agencies in the United States, Canada, and Australia. These listed chemicals are often referred to as existing chemicals. In the United States, TSCA requires EPA to compile, keep current, and publish a list of each chemical substance that is manufactured or processed in the United States. TSCA authorizes EPA to review chemicals already in commerce (existing chemicals) and chemicals yet to enter commerce (new chemicals). New chemicals are subject to premanufacture notice and EPA review, with some exceptions. This report focuses on existing chemical substances, which are not subject to new chemical notice and review requirements.[18]

Risk assessments characterize the potential adverse health effects of human exposures to environmental hazards, including chemicals, and are a key public policy tool for evaluating options for protecting public health and the environment. Risk management, as opposed to risk assessment, involves integrating risk assessment results with other information—such as economic information on the costs and benefits of mitigating the risk, technological information on the feasibility of managing the risk, and the concerns of various stakeholders—to decide what actions, if any, should be taken to protect public health. Examples of potential risk management actions include regulating how much of a chemical an entity may discharge into water or air, or creating guidelines for the use or disposal of specific chemicals.

Canada's CMP is run jointly by two Canadian federal departments—Environment Canada and Health Canada—and assesses existing chemicals and other substances listed on the country's Domestic Substances List[19] to determine which ones pose a risk to Canadians or the environment. One of the primary legislative tools used by the CMP to guide its efforts is CEPA 1999, which, according to a program overview document, provides for the assessment and management of substances to protect the environment and health of Canadians. According to Canadian officials, a risk assessment is required under CEPA 1999 to determine details on the hazardous qualities of a chemical or other substance and the specific ways people or the environment can be exposed. In 2006, the Canadian government launched the CMP, which assesses environmental and human health risks posed by chemical substances and develops and implements measures to prevent or manage those risks.[20]

Australia's IMAP framework is managed by the Australian Department of Health's National Industrial Chemicals Notification and Assessment Scheme (NICNAS), which conducts human health and environmental risk assessments of existing chemicals listed on the Australian Inventory of Chemical Substances (AICS).[21] According to its website, NICNAS aims to protect the Australian people and the environment by determining the risks to occupational health and safety, public health, and the environment that could be associated with the importation, manufacture, or use of industrial chemicals, and by maintaining a national standard for cosmetic products. Since 2012, NICNAS has used the IMAP framework to accelerate many of its assessments.

WHO's IARC aims to promote international collaboration in cancer research. According to the document that describes the scope and objectives of its monographs program, after receiving frequent requests for advice on the carcinogenic risk of chemicals, the agency's governing council recommended in 1970 that the agency prepare monographs on the evaluation of chemicals' carcinogenic risk to humans. The objective of the IARC Monographs Programme is to prepare and publish critical reviews and evaluations of evidence on the carcinogenicity of a wide range of human exposures.

WHO's IPCS aims to establish the scientific basis for the sound management of chemicals and to strengthen national capabilities for public safety, according to the program website. To do this, the program publishes a number of documents, including risk assessments, methodology documents, guidelines, and training documents. In 2013, the program also established the WHO Chemical Risk Assessment Network, which, among other things, provides an international forum for scientific and technical exchange.

FOREIGN PROGRAMS WE REVIEWED ASSESS THE HEALTH RISKS OF CHEMICALS USING SIMILAR ANALYTIC APPROACHES WHILE EMPHASIZING EITHER SCREENING ASSESSMENTS OR EXPERT REVIEW

In general, the programs we reviewed assess the human health risks of chemicals using similar analytic approaches, but they have some notable differences. Specifically, Canada and Australia's programs use screening assessments to characterize the risks of a large number of chemicals, and WHO's IARC Monographs Programme and IPCS emphasize expert review.[22]

Programs Use Similar Analytic Approaches to Conduct Assessments

In general, the programs we reviewed assess the human health risks of chemicals using similar analytic approaches. In terms of choosing what to assess, all four programs use specific criteria to determine priorities. For example, CEPA 1999 required the application of specific criteria to all substances on Canada's DSL to prioritize those for further assessment. These included chemicals that were inherently toxic to humans or nonhuman organisms and were persistent or bioaccumulative according to regulations.[23] In addition, each program works to identify basic information on a chemical—such as information on its properties and uses—before diving into deeper questions on human health risks. Each program also conducts literature searches to gather relevant information. Enclosure II provides a more detailed description of the risk assessment processes for each selected program.

Canada and Australia's Programs Emphasize Assessing a Large Number of Chemicals

Canada's CMP risk assessment activities for existing chemicals emphasize the assessment of thousands of chemicals and other substances from Canada's DSL. According to Canadian officials, these assessments look to determine the potential harm or danger a substance can cause to human health, the environment, or both, and the ways in which such harm or danger can happen. Pursuant to CEPA 1999, officials completed a process of prioritizing the roughly 23,000 chemicals and other substances on the DSL to identify those that warranted further assessment. According to a Canadian government website, that multiyear process was completed in 2006 and identified about 4,300 substances for further review. A Canadian government report showed that, among those, about 1,200 were identified based on human health concerns.[24] Canadian officials told us that, under the CMP, the government aims to address all of the approximately 4,300 substances by 2020 to determine whether they are toxic or capable of becoming toxic as defined by CEPA 1999.[25] According to CEPA 1999, officials shall apply the precautionary principle, which states that lack of full scientific certainty shall not be used as a reason for postponing action when a chemical or other substance may pose a threat of serious or irreversible damage. According to the CMP's spring 2015 progress report, the program is currently on track to meet its goals and reported that, as of June 2015, officials have completed screening assessments for about 2,700 substances (about 63 percent). Furthermore, since implementing the CMP, officials told us that they have added about 50 substances or groups of substances to CEPA 1999's List of Toxic Substances, which currently has 132 entries. Enclosure II provides a more detailed description of the risk assessment processes used by Canada's CMP.

According to the IMAP framework document, Australia's program also emphasizes the assessment of existing chemicals that have been used in Australia without prior assessment.[26] Modeled in part on Canada's CMP, officials told us that the IMAP framework prioritized for assessment between 2012 and 2016 about 3,000 chemicals[27] from the AICS, which officials told us included about 38,000 chemicals. The stated goal of the framework is to more rapidly assess chemicals, through screening assessments, to enhance information on whether the industrial use of selected chemicals poses an unreasonable risk to the public, workers, or the environment.[28] Officials told us that as of June 2015, they have assessed 3,185 unique chemicals on the AICS, completing their assessment goal well ahead of their 2016 schedule. Enclosure II provides a more detailed description of the risk assessment processes used by the IMAP framework.

WHO's IARC Monographs Programme and IPCS Emphasize Expert Review of Selected Chemicals

WHO's IARC Monographs Programme uses international experts to review selected chemicals and make determinations specifically about their human cancer risks through the use of published scientific principles and general operating procedures. Program officials appoint expert working groups to evaluate existing information on selected chemicals and other agents[29] and come to a determination about their carcinogenic risks to humans. Each working group is composed of internationally recognized experts chosen based on their knowledge and experience.[30] and meets for 7 to 8 days to discuss and finalize its evaluations, with the goal of forging consensus. According to its website, since 1971, the IARC Monographs Programme has assessed the carcinogenic risks of more than 900 chemicals and other agents. Enclosure II provides a more detailed description of the risk assessment processes used by this program.

WHO's IPCS also emphasizes using internationally recognized experts to review selected chemicals and make determinations about their human health risk, according to program guidelines.[31] Assessment drafts undergo peer review by internationally selected experts to help provide reasonable assurance of completeness and accuracy. As a specific example, to conduct assessments, an initial draft assessment is reviewed first by a panel of international peer reviewers selected for their scientific expertise, and revisions are expected to take peer review comments into account.[32] According to a program official, assessments are subject to approval by WHO senior management, but are published as the opinion of the panel of peer reviewing experts rather than as the official policy of WHO. According to its website and a program official, since 1976, IPCS has completed about 287 assessments. Enclosure II provides a more detailed description of the risk assessment processes used by WHO's IPCS.

CANADA HAS USED VARIOUS MEASURES TO MANAGE THE HUMAN HEALTH RISKS OF TOXIC CHEMICALS UNDER CEPA 1999

According to Canadian officials and Canadian government websites, Canada has used a variety of measures, including regulations, pollution prevention plan notices, and Significant New Activity provisions to manage the human health risks of chemicals determined to be toxic under CEPA 1999. For a substance determined to be toxic, Canadian officials told us that their current policy is to propose that the substance be added to CEPA 1999's List of Toxic Substances, if CEPA 1999 may be used to manage the risks identified. According to Canada's guide to CEPA 1999, the law requires that a draft and final risk management instrument be published in the *Canada Gazette* within 24 and 42 months, respectively, of the decision to propose addition to its List of Toxic Substances.[33] Measures used to manage risks associated with the 132 entries on CEPA 1999's List of Toxic Substances, according to relevant Environment Canada websites, include but are not limited to:

- Regulations. Canada has promulgated regulations (55 as of September 2015) that impose restrictions on an activity related to a chemical or other substance, or set limits on the concentrations of a chemical or substance that can be used, released to the environment, or be present in a product.[34]

- Pollution prevention plan notices. Pollution prevention plan notices (13 as of September 2015) require affected people (e.g. industrial facility operators) to prepare and implement a plan that outlines actions to prevent or minimize the creation or release of pollutants and waste.[35]
- Administrative agreements. Administrative agreements (2 as of September 2015) are work-sharing arrangements between the Canadian federal government and its provincial, territorial, or aboriginal governments to streamline efforts in administering CEPA 1999 regulations. The agreements usually cover topics such as inspections, monitoring, and reporting.[36] A Canadian official told us that implementing administrative agreements does not meet CEPA 1999 deadlines for drafting and finalizing risk management instruments.
- Significant New Activity Provisions (Orders and Notices). Significant New Activity provisions (28 as of September 2015 associated with the CMP), when issued, trigger an obligation for a person to provide the Canadian federal government with information about a substance when proposing to use, import, or manufacture the substance for a significant new activity.[37] The government then assesses the substance for potential risks to human health, the environment, or both. Officials told us that a Significant New Activity provision is essentially an obligation to report an activity (i.e., manufacture/import/use) that has not been conducted with the substance in the past or an existing one with a different quantity or in different circumstances that could affect the exposure pattern of the substance, allowing for future management as needed.
- Guidelines, objectives, and codes of practice. Guidelines, objectives, and codes of practice may be developed to give industries and regulators clear direction on how to reduce emissions, effluents, and wastes.[38] Guidelines are used, for example, to help limit releases of specified substances into the environment from works, undertakings, or activities. A code of practice is typically used, for example, to communicate detailed technical information.
- Environmental emergency plans under the Environmental Emergency Regulations. Persons who own or manage specified toxic chemicals and other substances at or above specified thresholds must (1) provide

required information on those substance(s) and their quantities and (2) prepare and implement environmental emergency plans that must address the types of emergencies that might reasonably occur, including both on-site and off-site consequences, and the associated prevention, preparedness, response, and recovery issues.[39] Persons must provide information on the quantity of the substance, facility location, a report that a plan has been prepared, and a notice that the plan has been implemented within specified time frames.

Enclosure III provides more detailed information on selected risk management measures used to address risks related to chemicals and other substances identified as toxic under CEPA 1999. For each selected measure, the enclosure includes one example of how that measure addressed a chemical or other substance determined to be toxic.

AGENCY AND THIRD-PARTY COMMENTS

We provided copies of this draft report to the Environmental Protection Agency (EPA) for review and comment, and to officials from Canada, Australia, and WHO for their review. EPA and officials from Canada, Australia, and WHO provided technical comments that we incorporated, as appropriate.

Sincerely yours,
J. Alfredo Gómez
Director, Natural Resources and Environment

Enclosure I

OBJECTIVES, SCOPE, AND METHODOLOGY

This report examined: (1) how selected foreign programs conduct risk assessment activities to understand the human health risks of certain chemicals, and (2) how Canada manages the human health risks of chemicals identified as toxic under the *Canadian Environmental Protection Act, 1999* (CEPA 1999).[40]

To identify foreign programs to review, we contacted Environmental Protection Agency (EPA) officials and academics with relevant expertise, and stakeholders in environmental and industry groups for their views on foreign programs that may produce quality chemical risk assessments. The four programs outside of the European Union that were identified most often by those we spoke with as having quality chemical assessment programs, and which we therefore selected, were: Canada, Australia, and the World Health Organization's (WHO) International Agency for Research on Cancer (IARC) Monographs Programme and International Programme on Chemical Safety (IPCS). Due to ongoing trade negotiations between the United States and the European Union, which include, among other things, negotiations concerning the coordination of their respective chemical regulatory regimes, we did not include European Union programs in the scope of this review. Within Canada, we focused on Canada's Chemicals Management Plan (CMP), which is run jointly by Environment Canada and Health Canada. Within Australia, we focused on the Inventory Multi-tiered Assessment and Prioritisation (IMAP) framework, implemented within Australia's National Industrial Chemicals Notification and Assessment Scheme (NICNAS). We focused on these programs because they are the main bodies in their countries conducting assessments of existing chemicals.[41] At WHO, we focused on the IARC Monographs Programme and IPCS because they were the specific programs suggested by those we contacted.

To determine how the foreign programs we selected conduct risk assessment activities to understand the human health risks of certain chemicals, we worked with representatives from each selected program: once for preliminary information, again to gather responses to a standard set of questions, and again as needed for follow-up questions. We also reviewed documents provided by officials from each program and information posted on their websites. This documentation included information on relevant laws, policies, and risk assessments. In addition, we talked with a number of academics with relevant knowledge on EPA and our selected programs' assessment processes. Last, we interviewed stakeholders representing an equal number of environmental and industry groups to understand their views on selected programs' practices and processes. We identified these stakeholders by consulting our prior work and by soliciting input from EPA officials and academics with relevant knowledge. We then selected three stakeholders representing environmental groups and three representing industry groups, choosing first those for whom we had received at least two recommendations and then contacting all others and interviewing those who responded first. The views of these particular environmental and industry groups cannot be generalized to all other environmental and industry groups, but they provided valuable insights to our work. We did not evaluate the effectiveness of any of the programs described. In addition, we did not evaluate the scientific content or quality of selected foreign programs' assessments. We did not compare any elements of these programs to EPA's Integrated Risk Information System (IRIS) Program or other EPA chemical assessment programs.

To determine how Canada manages the human health risks of chemicals identified as toxic under CEPA 1999, we met with relevant officials from Canada and reviewed documentation provided by those officials and published on their website. We chose to focus on Canada— rather than on all selected programs—for a few reasons. First, Canada's CEPA 1999 is regularly discussed in the debate on reforming the Toxic Substances Control Act (TSCA) in the United States. In addition, Environment Canada and Health Canada, which run Canada's CMP, are the only programs in our study that also conduct risk management activities. According to Australian officials, NICNAS is not responsible for managing chemical risks; instead, Australian officials told us that other Australian federal, provincial, territorial, and aboriginal governments conduct risk management work. WHO's IARC Monographs Programme and IPCS also do not conduct risk management work, which is the purview of WHO member countries. To select sample chemicals to demonstrate how chemicals are managed as discussed in enclosure III, we first identified four types of risk management measures that may be used by Canada to manage risks associated with chemicals on CEPA 1999's List of Toxic Substances. We chose to focus on these four types because officials have created readily available lists of the chemicals associated with those types of actions on Environment Canada's websites. In addition, in the case of Significant New Activity provisions, officials told us that it is the risk management measure they use most often to address substances determined to be toxic. For each of these risk management measures, we used lists of chemicals associated with those measures as presented by Environment Canada's websites. We then randomly ordered those lists. Starting with the first randomly-ordered chemical, we determined (1) whether it was on CEPA 1999's List of Toxic Substances and (2) if it was managed for human health reasons— the focus of this report—as opposed to environmental reasons. If those two things were true, we used it as an example. We chose to report on one example for each type of management measure. We did not compare what we learned about Canada to how EPA or other U.S. agencies manage the human health risks of chemicals.

We conducted this performance audit from March 2014 to October 2015 in accordance with generally accepted government auditing standards. Those standards require that we plan and perform the audit to obtain sufficient, appropriate evidence to provide a reasonable basis for our findings and conclusions based on our audit objectives. We believe that the evidence obtained provides a reasonable basis for our findings and conclusions based on our audit objectives.

Enclosure II

INFORMATION FROM CANADA, AUSTRALIA, AND THE WORLD HEALTH ORGANIZATION ABOUT SELECTED RISK ASSESSMENT PROCESSES

A description of the risk assessment processes for existing substances used by programs implementing Canada's Chemicals Management Plan (CMP), Australia's Inventory Multi-tiered Assessment and Prioritisation (IMAP) framework, and the World Health Organization's (WHO) International Agency for Research on Cancer (IARC) Monographs Programme and International Programme on Chemical Safety (IPCS) follows. For each program, we examined

- the main determination[42] made by each program's assessments;
- the criteria for choosing which chemicals to assess; and
- involvement by external experts, stakeholders, and/or the public.

1. Canada's CMP

Main Determination Made by Each Program's Assessments

As part of its CMP, officials in Canada conduct screening assessments to determine whether chemicals and other substances on its Domestic Substances List[43] are toxic according to the definition set forth in the *Canadian Environmental Protection Act, 1999* (CEPA 1999).[44] CEPA 1999 defines a substance as toxic if it is entering or may enter the environment in a quantity or concentration or under conditions that (a) have or may have an immediate or long-term harmful effect on the environment or its biological diversity; (b) constitute or may constitute a danger to the environment on which life depends; or (c) constitute or may constitute a danger in Canada to human life or health. Program officials told us that assessments incorporate several elements, including information on each chemical's physical and chemical properties, uses and sources, hazard identification, exposure assessment, and risk characterization. They also told us they use comprehensive information gathering approaches to support their assessments, and that they review chemicals for their human health effects of concern to the general public rather than for specific populations such as workers in a particular industry. They also told us that they focus their review on what would be considered "reasonable, foreseeable" uses. If an assessment determines that a substance is toxic under CEPA 1999, officials may take one of three actions: (1) add the substance to CEPA 1999's List of Toxic Substances[45] and, if applicable, to CEPA 1999's Virtual Elimination List;[46] (2) add the substance to CEPA 1999's Priority Substances List, which identifies substances that must undergo further assessment within five years; or (3) take no further action. In practice, officials told us that their policy has been to take action on chemicals by adding them to CEPA 1999's List of Toxic Substances, which then can lead to risk management actions, including regulations, although exceptions exist where action is not taken under CEPA 1999 authority. According to CEPA 1999, in interpreting the results of a screening assessment, officials shall apply the precautionary principle, which states that lack of full scientific certainty shall not be used as a reason for postponing action when a chemical or other substance may pose a threat of serious or irreversible damage.

CEPA 1999 also allows officials to review decisions from other jurisdictions. Specifically, were Canada's Minister of the Environment to receive information that another government[47] has specifically prohibited or substantially restricted a substance for environmental or health reasons, the federal Ministers of the Environment and Health must review that decision. The review is to determine whether the substance is toxic or capable of becoming toxic according to CEPA 1999, unless the decision relates to a substance the only use of which in Canada is regulated under another Act of Parliament that provides for environmental and health protection. Program officials told us that they have implemented a process to conduct this work. According to Canada's guide to CEPA 1999, this process allows Canada to benefit from the sharing of scientific data, the capacity of other governments, and efforts by others to develop risk management measures.

Program officials told us that prior to implementation of the CMP in 2006, assessments were largely identified under their Priority Substances Assessment Program. There have been two priority substances lists (PSL) associated with this program—PSL1 and PSL2. Under CEPA 1999, PSL substances are required to be assessed within 5 years of their addition. PSL1 covered 44 substances, and PSL2, which covered 25 substances, was derived from recommendations made by an expert advisory panel.[48]

Criteria for Choosing What to Assess

According to Canada's guide to CEPA 1999, between passage of the act and 2006, the program went through a process to prioritize all of the approximately 23,000 chemicals and other substances on the Domestic Substances List to choose which should be further assessed (officials referred to this as a 'categorization exercise'). To do so, pursuant to CEPA 1999 officials identified those substances that (1) are persistent or bioaccumulative according to the regulations and inherently toxic to human beings or nonhuman organisms, as determined by laboratory or other studies; or (2) may present to individuals in Canada the greatest potential for exposure.[49] This process resulted in about 4,300 chemicals and other substances being prioritized for further assessment, about 1,200 of which were for human health reasons.

In 2014, officials in Environment Canada and Health Canada formalized an approach to prioritize existing chemicals and other substances for further assessment.[50] According to the document outlining this approach, the objective of ongoing prioritization is to selectively identify substances for which there are indications that the substance should be considered as a new priority for assessment or further work. This could include identifying chemicals or other substances that had previously been assessed. The document also states priority setting decisions are based on a set of guiding principles and considerations, such as whether new information gathered is relevant and scientifically reliable, and whether recently acquired information refutes a key assumption in a past decision or recommendation. Officials told us that they intend to go through a process to consider new priorities on a yearly basis, but that assessments prioritized using this new approach may not begin in earnest until they have completed their work to address the approximately 4,300 substances they have already committed to review by 2020. Officials told us that they can also determine new priorities (using criteria such as new scientific evidence) on an ad hoc basis.

Involvement by External Experts, Stakeholders, or the Public

To involve stakeholders or the public during the assessment process, officials use a variety of mechanisms. A program document identifies stakeholders as representatives of industries and industry associations, nongovernmental organizations, environmental and health groups, and labor and consumer organizations. The document also states that officials involve stakeholders at several points in the assessment process, including during the process of identifying which chemicals and other substances to assess, problem formulation/issue identification, and expert peer review. Officials also publish notices in the *Canada Gazette*[51] when assessments are available for public comment. Canadian government officials told us that industry stakeholders are sometimes involved in the assessment development process when officials require industry members to provide data on the properties and uses of specific chemicals.[52] Officials told us they also obtain input from standing committees composed of stakeholders and experts such as through the CMP Science Committee and CMP Stakeholder Advisory Committee.

To involve external experts, a program document states that draft assessments are sent for scientific review to a variety of Canadian and international experts, selected from academia, government, industry, and/or environmental groups. A revised report is subsequently prepared, taking into account the comments of these expert reviewers. Officials told us they also engage experts to review full draft assessments or specific aspects of an assessment on an as-needed basis.

According to Canada's guide to CEPA 1999, if stakeholders or others are unsatisfied with the outcome of an assessment, they may file a notice of objection and request that a Board of Review be established to inquire into the nature and extent of the danger posed by the substance in respect of which the decision is made. Depending on the nature of the information received, Canada's Minister of the Environment then determines if further discussions or a Board of Review are warranted. If the Minister establishes a Board of Review, the board then inquires into the nature and extent of the danger posed by the substance that is the subject of the order or the proposed regulation. According to officials from Health Canada, they have received about 10 requests for a Board of Review in their history of conducting assessments, and the Minister of the Environment has approved 1 request. Officials told us that these requests can be granted based on receipt of what they understand to be "significant" new information.

2. Australia's IMAP Framework

Main Determination Made by Each Program's Assessments

Based on the program's website, Australia's IMAP framework is used by the National Industrial Chemicals Notification and Assessment Scheme (NICNAS), and works to identify whether industrial chemicals[53] from the Australian Inventory of Chemical Substances (AICS)[54] are likely to pose an unreasonable risk to workers, the general public, and/or the environment, and—if so—what recommendations should be made to reduce that risk. According to the IMAP framework's main policy document, if an assessment concludes that a chemical may pose an unreasonable risk to the general public, workers, or the environment, the assessment includes recommendations to manage those risks.[55] According to an Australian policy document, assessments may recommend that chemicals be placed on Australia's Poisons Standard—a compilation of decisions recommending restrictions or prohibitions to manage public health risks for certain chemicals and medicines, among other things.[56] According to the documentation and NICNAS officials, Australian state and territory governments are responsible for imposing legislative controls on the supply and use of such chemicals. For example, according to NICNAS officials, under the Poisons Standard, chemicals may be subjected to labeling requirements, prohibition of some or all uses, or both. To improve worker health, assessments may recommend adding information about a chemical to Australia's Hazardous Chemical Information List to facilitate getting the proper information on safety data sheets and labels, which are provided to help industry members understand health and safety hazards.[57]

According to its main policy document, the IMAP framework was created following a review of NICNAS' program to review existing chemicals between 2003 and 2006. The review examined the program against emerging national and international trends to determine if it was sufficiently responsive and flexible in meeting national needs and the priorities of NICNAS' stakeholders, while ensuring continued efficient and effective use of resources. The review's major concerns were that (1) most chemicals on the AICS were initially listed based on their history of use, and most had not since been assessed for their effects on human health and the environment, and (2) the current assessment process for those chemicals was not flexible enough to respond adequately, or in a resource-efficient manner, to stakeholder concerns. Based on those concerns, NICNAS began working with stakeholders and technical experts in 2008 to develop a framework to more quickly prioritize and assess chemicals on the AICS. One key element in this framework includes using overseas data to reduce duplication of assessment effort and increase efficiency.

Criteria for Choosing What to Assess

According to its main policy document, the IMAP framework is currently in its first stage of implementation and used three criteria to prioritize for assessment 3,000 chemicals on the AICS during this first stage: those that have (1) exposure data available to NICNAS, (2) been identified as a concern or for which action has been taken overseas, or (3) been detected in umbilical cord blood. Officials used various sources of information to consider these criteria. For example, to prioritize chemicals that have been identified as a concern or for which action has been taken overseas, officials used information on chemicals assessed by Canada's CMP and chemicals with U.S. Environmental Protection Agency action plans.[58] To prioritize chemicals that have been detected in umbilical cord blood, program documentation indicates that officials used information from a study by international sources.

Involvement by External Experts, Stakeholders, or the Public

According to the IMAP framework's main policy document, officials consult with external experts, stakeholders, or the public using a variety of mechanisms, such as publishing information on draft assessments for public comment in the *NICNAS Bulletin*.[59] According to program officials, industry members also have the opportunity to provide voluntary information prior to, during, or after the assessment process. Also according to program officials, working closely with other international regulatory agencies has also contributed significantly to the effectiveness of the program. Officials also obtain input from standing committees composed of representatives from industry, community organizations, other government entities, and experts. Specifically, according to program officials, the program seeks input from the NICNAS Strategic Consultative Committee, which comprises representatives of industry and community organizations. In addition, program officials told us that consultations may also be undertaken with other stakeholders, such as academics and government risk management agencies.

3. WHO's IARC Monographs Programme, as Outlined in the Program's Preamble[60]

To guide its work, the IARC Monographs Programme uses a published Preamble document that serves as a statement of scientific principles and general operating procedures. An IARC official also told us that the Preamble establishes transparent, standard procedures for selecting and reviewing evidence and making a final evaluation.

Main Determination Made by Each Program's Assessments

WHO's IARC Mongraphs Programme makes determinations about the likelihood that selected agents—defined as specific chemicals, groups of related chemicals, complex mixtures, occupational or environmental exposures, cultural or behavioral practices, biological organisms and physical agents—cause cancer in humans using five categories ranging from "the agent is carcinogenic to humans" to "the agent is probably not carcinogenic to humans."[61] The Preamble states that a cancer 'hazard' is an agent that is capable of causing cancer under some circumstances, while a cancer 'risk' is an estimate of the carcinogenic effects expected from exposure to a cancer hazard. The Preamble goes on to state that the IARC Monographs Programme evaluates cancer hazards, even when risks are very low at current exposure levels, because new uses or unforeseen exposures could engender risks that are significantly higher. According to the Preamble, assessments are used by national and international authorities to conduct further assessment or decide among alternative options for public health decisions, among other things. Because assessments from the IARC Monographs Programme represent only one part of the information on which public health decisions may be based, and public health options may vary from one situation to another and from country to country, assessments do not include specific risk management recommendations, which are the responsibility of individual governments or other international organizations.

Criteria for Choosing What to Assess

According to the program's Preamble document, the IARC Monographs Programme uses two criteria to prioritize chemicals and other agents for assessment: (1) evidence of human exposure and (2) some evidence or suspicion of carcinogenicity. The program periodically convenes an advisory group to recommend topics for assessment. Advisory group documentation stated that the program convenes such advisory groups to ensure that IARC assessments reflect the current state of priorities for public health. The advisory group met in April 2014 and recommended 24 types of chemicals and other agents as high priorities for review. The advisory group also recommended 20 chemicals and other agents as medium priorities for review.

Involvement by External Experts, Stakeholders, or the Public

To involve experts, stakeholders, and the public, the program uses a variety of strategies. To involve experts outside of those serving as working group members, officials invite what they call "specialists"—experts who are deemed to have critical knowledge and experience but have a real or apparent conflict of interests—to participate in working group meetings. Invited specialists are asked to contribute their knowledge and experience during discussions, and may also contribute text on noninfluential issues in a monograph's section on exposure. Invited specialists do not chair meetings or draft text that pertains to the description or interpretation of cancer data, or participate in making final evaluation decisions. To involve interested stakeholders, program policy allows representatives of national and international health agencies to attend meetings. In addition, according to a program official, individuals wishing to be observers may request to attend meetings, and the program invites a limited number of such observers who have relevant scientific credentials. Observers are invited with attention given to achieving a balance of observers from constituencies with differing perspectives. According to a program official, neither representatives nor observers draft any text for a monograph or participate in evaluation decisions. Also according to a program official, the program involves the public by soliciting public nominations for chemicals or other agents to assess. The program does not solicit public input on draft assessments.

4. WHO's IPCS

Main Determination Made by Each Program's Assessments

According to program guidelines, WHO's IPCS makes determinations about the health impacts of chemicals by a process of assessment that aims to provide a consensus scientific description of the risks of chemical exposure. To do this, authors usually base their work on an existing national, regional, or international review, or a review in preparation to provide a concise summary of the information considered critical for risk characterization. Alternatively, a full assessment may be written by an expert. Assessments include "sample" risk characterizations that, according to program guidance, are intended to provide examples of how risks of certain populations might be characterized, based upon the toxicological and exposure information presented in the assessment. Sample risk characterizations do not necessarily represent all possible exposure situations, but they are provided as example and guidance only. As with WHO's IARC Monographs Programme, a program official told us that assessments from the IPCS do not provide specific risk management recommendations, but may inform further assessment or risk management measures made by WHO member governments or others.

Criteria for Choosing What to Assess

According to program officials, due to resource limitations, the program currently reviews chemicals primarily to satisfy obligations under international conventions, such as the Stockholm Convention.[62] For example, in 2011, the program published an assessment on the human health effects of dichlorodiphenyltrichloroethane (DDT) with specific advice to the Conference of the Parties to the Stockholm Convention about the use of DDT in controlling mosquitoes that spread malaria.[63] According to its annual activity report, the program reviews the literature annually to consider whether the assessment should be revisited. To date, according to this report, these literature reviews have not suggested that a revision is needed.[64] Prior to its current resource limitations, program guidelines state that the program used specific criteria to prioritize chemicals for assessment, such as (1) probability of exposure and/or, (2) significant toxicity. Additional criteria included whether a chemical: (3) was of transboundary concern, (4) was of concern to a range of countries (developed, developing, and those with economies in transition) for possible risk management, (5) had significant international trade, (6) had a high production volume, or (7) had a dispersive use. Special emphasis was placed on avoiding duplication of effort by WHO and other international organizations.

Involvement by Experts, Stakeholders or the Public

To involve experts, program guidelines state that the program works with a primary author on a first draft, which is often based on an existing national, regional, or international review. This primary author usually prepares a first draft based on these reviews, or on a review in preparation using a standard outline created by IPCS to encourage consistency in form. The draft is then reviewed first by IPCS officials to ensure that it meets specified criteria. Following that, the draft undergoes an international peer review of scientists.

Primary authors are required to take peer reviewers' comments into account and revise their draft, as appropriate.

- For one type of IPCS assessment called a Concise International Chemical Assessment Document (CICAD), the resulting second draft then moves to a second reviewing board—called the Final Review Board—with a role of, among other things, (1) ensuring that each assessment has been subjected to an appropriate and thorough peer review and (2) providing guidance on how to resolve any remaining issues that an author may not have adequately addressed. A program official told us that the Final Review Board will meet for 2 to 3 days to review and finalize the assessment.
- For types of IPCS assessments not considered by a Final Review Board, which may include IPCS' Environmental Health Criteria (EHC) documents, an official told us that WHO convenes a meeting of invited experts to consider peer review comments and agree on the final version of the assessment.

Assessments are also subject to approval by WHO senior management but are published on the basis of being the opinion of a group of experts rather than as the official policy of the organization.

According to a program official, to involve stakeholders and the public, program officials accept nominations on which chemicals to assess from anyone. In addition, they solicit stakeholder and public comments on draft assessments through publication on the program's website and through e-mail to those on the program's mailing list. Recent assessments received between 15 and 30 such comments, usually submitted by academics, industry stakeholders, and nongovernmental organizations. For applicable assessments, the Final Review Board is responsible for considering these comments as they deliberate.

Enclosure III

Selected Risk Management Measures for Chemicals Identified as Toxic Under CEPA 1999

In deciding which risk management measures to use to prevent and control risk associated with chemicals or substances identified as toxic under the *Canadian Environmental Protection Act, 1999* (CEPA 1999),[65] Canadian government officials told us that when they examine risk management measures, they consider potential effectiveness of a potential measure, along with whether it is proportional to the risks posed by any given chemical or substance. In addition, Canadian officials told us that they consider international agreements and their obligations under those agreements when deciding which risk management measures to pursue.

According to Canada's guide to CEPA 1999, risk management measures for chemicals on CEPA 1999's List of Toxic Substances are developed through a process that aims to involve stakeholders.[66] When selecting a specific risk management strategy for a chemical determined to be toxic under CEPA 1999, the government outlines the proposed approach for managing the risks to the environment and human health using risk assessments and other information to help determine which measure or measures would best address those risks. Initially, all available risk management measures are considered, including regulatory provisions of other governments and voluntary approaches. These may also include risk management measures that are already in place such as pollution prevention plans, administrative agreements, and Significant New Activity provisions.[67] Risk management measures may focus on any aspect of the chemical or other substance's life cycle—from the research and development stage through manufacture, use, storage, transportation, and ultimate disposal.

This enclosure focuses on four types of risk management measures used by Canada to address the risks posed by chemicals and other substances determined to be toxic. For each type of measure, this enclosure includes one example of how that measure addressed a chemical or other substance determined to be toxic under CEPA 1999.

Regulations

Canada has promulgated regulations on chemicals and other substances that impose restrictions on a chemical-related activity, or set limits on the concentrations of a chemical, or other substance that can be used, released to the environment, or be present in a product.[68] According to an Environment Canada website, as of September 2015, there were 55 regulations associated with chemicals and other substances determined to be toxic under CEPA 1999 and its predecessor CEPA 1988.[69] They cover a wide range of activities, chemicals, and emissions.

One group of substances that is managed in Canada through regulations is volatile organic compounds (VOC). VOCs are chemicals that are emitted as gases from natural sources—such as trees—as well as from anthropogenic (human-caused) sources—such as motor vehicles, paints, solvents, fuels, and other products. VOCs are also primary precursors to the formation of ground level ozone and particulate matter, which are the main constituents of smog. In Canada, human health concerns related to VOC emissions stem from: the transportation sector; the use of consumer and commercial products that contain solvents; some commercial and industrial processes; and residential wood combustion.[70] To manage risks associated with this group of substances, Canada has developed risk management measures to address those concerns, including promulgating its VOC Concentration Limits for Architectural Coatings Regulations (the VOC regulation).[71]

According to an Environment Canada website, the purpose of the VOC regulation is to protect the environment and health of Canadians from the effects of air pollution by reducing VOC emissions.[72] A draft of the proposed VOC regulation was made available for public comment on April 26, 2008 and citizens were given the opportunity to file comments. In addition, the National Advisory Committee under CEPA 1999 was given the opportunity to provide its advice.[73] The VOC regulation indicates that, while substances regulated by other acts are excluded from the VOC regulation, it provides sufficient protection to the environment and health. According to an Environment Canada website, the regulation sets a maximum VOC concentration limit in 53 categories of architectural coatings.[74] In addition, the regulation defines methods for determining VOC concentrations and other test methods, labelling requirements, and record keeping.

Pollution Prevention Plan Notices

CEPA 1999 authorizes the Canadian Minister of the Environment to issue notices requiring affected people (e.g., industrial facility operators) to prepare and implement pollution prevention plans for substances or group of substances specified on CEPA 1999's List of Toxic Substances. CEPA 1999 defines pollution prevention as "the use of processes, practices, materials, products, substances or energy that avoid or minimize the creation of pollutants and waste and reduce the overall risk to the environment or human health." Pollution prevention involves determining where waste is generated to identify how best to eliminate or reduce it at the source.

According to an Environment Canada website on pollution prevention plans, the notices are published in the *Canada Gazette* and do not provide details about them, but rather state that affected people may prepare a plan in the form that makes the most sense for their facility, as long as the plan meets specific requirements.[75] Those requirements can include that the plan addresses the specific "factors to consider" outlined in the notice and complies with the timelines established in the notice. In addition, the website has outlined ways for the plan to be most effective, including that it

- designate a senior manager who will be accountable for the plan;
- clearly state the risk management objectives for the plan;
- create a schedule for meeting the objectives of the plan; and
- create a plan for measuring, tracking, and evaluating the success of the selected options and for implementing corrective and preventative measures, among others.[76]

According to an Environment Canada website on pollution prevention plans, as of September 2015, there were 13 published notices in the *Canada Gazette* requiring pollution prevention plans: (1) siloxane d4 in industrial effluent, (2) the resin and synthetic rubber manufacturing sector, (3) bisphenol A (BPA), (4) the polyurethane and other foam sector (except polystyrene), (5) mercury releases from dental amalgam waste, (6) mercury releases from mercury switches in end-of-life vehicles, (7) base metals smelters and refineries and zinc plants, (8) wood preservation facilities, (9) textile mills that use wet processing, (10) nonylphenol and its ethoxylates, (11) inorganic chloramines and chlorinated wastewater effluents, (12) dichloromethane, and (13) acrylonitrile.[77] Pollution prevention is about avoiding the creation of pollution and waste, rather than trying to clean it up or manage it after the fact. A pollution prevention website states that waste has traditionally been managed through treatment, recycling, control equipment, and landfilling—referred to in Canada as "end-of-pipe" processes. Pollution prevention involves determining where waste is generated to identify how best to eliminate or reduce it at the source.

Canada published a pollution prevention planning notice in the *Canada Gazette* in 2003 for acrylonitrile.[78] Acrylonitrile is a volatile, flammable, colorless liquid with a weakly pungent odor.

According to an Environment Canada fact sheet, there are no known natural sources of acrylonitrile. It is not produced in Canada, and the majority of acrylonitrile is used in the chemical industry to produce synthetic rubbers and polymers. In 2008, according to Environment Canada, an estimated 5,900 metric tons of acrylonitrile was imported in Canada— all of which was imported from the United States.[79]

The notice required that any person who owned or operated a facility that manufactured synthetic rubber—where such manufacture and use of acrylonitrile that resulted in its release to the environment—to prepare and implement a pollution prevention plan.[80] One Canadian facility issued such a plan in 2004 that included four different pollution prevention techniques: (1) on-site recovery, reuse, and recycling; (2) equipment/process modifications; (3) spill and leak preventions; and (4) good operating practices. According to the *Final Report: Pollution Prevention Planning and Acrylonitrile*, implementation of the acrylonitrile pollution prevention plan helped the Canadian company significantly reduce releases of this chemical into the environment. In July 2009, the *Final Report* stated that the facility took actions to prevent pollution at the source, noting that the pollution prevention plan had been fully implemented.

Administrative Agreements

According to Environment Canada documents, including Canada's guide to CEPA 1999, administrative agreements are work-sharing arrangements between the Canadian federal government and its provincial, territorial, or aboriginal governments to streamline efforts in administering CEPA 1999 regulations.[81] The agreements usually cover topics such as inspections, monitoring, and reporting. A Canadian official told us that implementing administrative agreements does not meet CEPA 1999 deadlines for drafting and finalizing risk management instruments. As of September 2015, there were 2 administrative agreements.

According to an Environment Canada website on administrative agreements, the Canadian federal government currently has an agreement with the provincial government of Saskatchewan covering seven CEPA 1999 regulations.[82] According to the website, the agreement with Saskatchewan has been in force since September 15, 1994 and covers regulations related to the pulp and paper mill sector, ozone depleting substances and products, chlorobiphenyls, federal mobile polychlorinated biphenyl (PCB) treatment and destruction, and storage of PCB material. This working agreement between the Canadian federal government and the provincial government of Saskatchewan notes that both entities are committed to maximizing cooperation and coordination in their respective compliance and enforcement programs. Specifically, the Canada-Saskatchewan administrative agreement recognizes that sustainable development and social well-being depend upon the preservation of a high standard of environmental quality. To implement the administrative agreement, a management committee was established that is responsible for ensuring collaboration among activities including those related to monitoring, research, spills and releases, publications, and conferences.

Significant New Activity Provisions (Orders and Notices)

According to an Environment Canada website, Significant New Activity provisions, when issued, trigger an obligation for a person to provide the Canadian federal government with information about a substance when proposing to use, import, or manufacture the substance for a significant new activity.[83] The website goes on to state that the government then assesses the substance for potential risks to human health, the environment, or both. Officials told us that a Significant New Activity provision is essentially an obligation to report an activity—of manufacture, import, or use—that has not been conducted with the substance in the past or an existing one with a different quantity or in different circumstances that could affect the exposure pattern of the substance, allowing for future management, as needed. In addition, if an individual or corporation wants to manufacture, import, or use the substance in a way that is captured by the Significant New Activity provision, Canada requires that specific additional information is provided by the individual or corporation; a risk assessment be performed; and, if necessary, risk management measures be implemented by the government prior to any new activity. Officials told us that they have used Significant New Activity provisions to address substances found to be toxic as part of their Chemicals Management Plan (used 28 times as part of the Chemicals Management Plan as of September 2015).[84] They stated that because current exposures were negligible or well managed for these substances and because there is a reasonable suspicion that new activities with respect to these substances may result in new or increased risks to the environment or human health, Canadian officials felt the best course of action was to require notification by the individual or corporation if its uses for those chemicals changed.

According to a Canadian government website, Environment Canada and Health Canada are undertaking a review of Significant New Activity Orders and Notices currently in place under CEPA 1999[85] since publication of the first Significant New Activity provisions in 2001. This is because Canadian policies and procedures have changed, particularly with respect to the nature and scope of a Significant New Activity provision, as well as the criteria used to identify what a "significant new activity" entails. The website states that the review is being undertaken to ensure that Significant New Activity provisions are in step with current information, policies, and approaches. The resulting changes are expected to provide greater clarity of scope and improve ease of compliance by industry.[86]

C.I. Pigment Red 104, also known as molybdate orange is an example of a chemical that Canada manages with a Significant New Activity provision.[87] This pigment is part of the chemical grouping UVCB substances (substances of Unknown or Variable Composition, Complex Reaction Products, or Biological Materials), which means that its chemical composition is not precisely known, among other things.[88] According to the *Canada Gazette*, C.I. Pigment Red 104 is used in plastic formulation for commercial applications and export; commercial, nonconsumer paints and coatings; and in a very limited number of commercial printing inks or coatings used for plastics and certain outdoor applications such as commercial identification decals. According to the *Canada Gazette*, this substance was reported to be manufactured in and imported into Canada in 2006.[89] According to the *Canada Gazette*, on January 31, 2009, a notice summarizing the scientific considerations of a final screening assessment for C.I. Pigment Red 104 was published in the *Canada Gazette*.[90] The final screening assessment report concluded that "C.I. Pigment Red 104 is entering or may be entering the environment in a quantity or a concentration or under conditions that constitute or may constitute a danger in Canada to human life or health."[91]

The Significant New Activity provision applicable to C.I. Pigment Red 104 refers to its use as a component of commercial printing inks, or as a component of decals in industrial or commercial applications, among other things. The *Canada Gazette* states that at least 180 days before the day on which the quantity of C.I. Pigment Red 104 exceeds 100 kilograms in any one calendar year, the Canadian government must be provided, among other things: (1) a description of the significant new activity in relation to the substance; (2) the anticipated annual quantity of the substance to be used for the significant new activity; and (3) if known, the three sites in Canada where the greatest quantity of the substance is anticipated to be used or processed and the estimated quantity by site.[92]

End Notes

[1] The WHO directs and coordinates international health within the United Nations' system. The United States is one of 194 WHO member states.

[2] Risk assessments typically include four components: hazard identification, dose-response assessment, exposure assessment, and risk characterization. According to their representatives, WHO's IARC Monographs Programme produces the hazard identification

component of an assessment, while the other three programs produce all four components. Other foreign programs, including those in the European Union, also conduct risk assessments. Due to ongoing trade negotiations between the United States and the European Union that address, among other things, coordination of chemical regulatory regimes, we did not include European Union entities in our review.

[3] GAO, Chemical Assessments: Low Productivity and New Interagency Review Process Limit the Usefulness and Credibility of EPA's Integrated Risk Information System, GAO-08-440 (Washington, D.C.: Mar. 7, 2008); Chemical Assessments: Challenges Remain with EPA's Integrated Risk Information System Program, GAO-12-42 (Washington, D.C.: Dec. 9, 2011); and Chemical Assessments: An Agencywide Strategy May Help EPA Address Unmet Needs for Integrated Risk Information System Assessments, GAO-13-369 (Washington, D.C.: May 10, 2013).

[4] GAO, High-Risk Series: An Update, GAO-09-271 (Washington, D.C.: January 2009).

[5] Toxic Substances Control Act, Pub. L. No. 94-469, 90 Stat. 2003 (1976).

[6] GAO-13-369, and High-Risk Series: An Update, GAO-15-290 (Washington, D.C.: February 2015).

[7] Suggestions included, for example, that (1) draft assessments undergo rigorous editing to substantially reduce the volume of text, and (2) critical studies be thoroughly evaluated with standardized approaches. National Research Council of the National Academies, Review of the Environmental Protection Agency's Draft IRIS Assessment of Formaldehyde (Washington, D.C.: National Academies Press, 2011).

[8] According to EPA, RapidTox is under development to provide information in fiscal years 2016-2109 on data poor chemicals (i.e. those that are lacking the data EPA needs to make risk management decisions) and to reduce the time, cost and/or uncertainty of risk-based chemical management decisions. The goal is to deliver RapidTox assessments for large numbers of data poor chemicals and provide a range of information related to hazard, chemical properties, fate and transport, and exposure. The information will include data from traditional sources when available, as well as new data being developed by EPA. The project will investigate methods to integrate and distill data to support decisions. The first case study, developed in collaboration with EPA's Office of Chemical Safety and Pollution Prevention, is expected to have results in the fourth quarter of fiscal year 2016. Two additional case studies are being explored with the Office of Solid Waste and Emergency Response and the Office of Water for implementation in late 2016 and early 2017.

[9] GAO, Toxic Substances: EPA Has Increased Efforts to Assess and Control Chemicals but Could Strengthen Its Approach, GAO-13-249 (Washington, D.C.: Mar. 22, 2013).

[10] As we reported, even when EPA has information on existing chemicals, the agency has said that it has had difficulty demonstrating that harmful chemicals pose an unreasonable risk and that they should be banned or have limits placed on their use. In order to regulate an existing chemical under TSCA, EPA must find that there is a reasonable basis to conclude that the chemical presents or will present an unreasonable risk of injury to health or the environment. Further, the regulation must apply the least burdensome requirement that will adequately protect against the risk. See GAO, Chemical Regulation: Options Exist to Improve EPA's Ability to Assess Health Risks and Manage Its Chemical Review Program, GAO-05-458 (Washington, D.C.: June 13, 2005) and GAO-15-290.

[11] Those five chemicals or chemical classes are polychlorinated biphenyls (PCB), fully halogenated chlorofluoroalkanes, dioxin, asbestos, and hexavalent chromium. One of these TSCA actions was overturned in court, while some others were superseded by later EPA

regulations issued under other laws. For further information about these chemicals and chemical classes, see GAO-05-458, appendix V, 58-60.

[12] For example, in June 2015, the House of Representatives passed H.R. 2576, TSCA Modernization Act of 2015, which would amend TSCA's provisions governing chemical testing, regulation, and data disclosure. The bill is pending in the Senate.

[13] GAO-15-290.

[14] Canadian Environmental Protection Act, 1999, S.C. 1999, c. 3, as amended (Can.) [hereinafter CEPA 1999].

[15] Canadian officials use the term "screening assessments" to describe the assessments they conduct under the CMP. Australia's IMAP assessments are referred to simply as "assessments." For the purposes of this report, we use the term "screening assessments" to describe both.

[16] According to Canada's guide to CEPA 1999, a substance includes any distinguishable kind of organic or inorganic matter, whether animate or inanimate, that is capable of being released as a single substance, an effluent, emission, waste or a mixture into the Canadian environment. Environment Canada, A Guide to Understanding the Canadian Environmental Protection Act, 1999 (Dec. 10 2004), accessed July 27, 2015, http://www.ec.gc.ca/lcpe-cepa/E00B5BD8-13BC-4FBF-9B74-1013AD5FFC05/Guide04_e.pdf.

[17] Substances that meet the definition of toxic under CEPA 1999 can be placed on the List of Toxic Substances. A substance's presence on this list alone does not impose specific management measures on the use of the substance. The recommendation for a chemical's addition to this list, however, triggers statutory obligations that generally require the Canadian government to contemplate and potentially issue chemical management measures for that chemical within specified periods.

[18] In addition, this report does not discuss chemicals and other substances that are regulated under other laws including certain nuclear materials, pesticides, foods, food additives, tobacco, and cosmetics.

[19] According to a program review document, Health Canada is responsible for assessing human health risks, and Environment Canada is responsible for assessment of ecological risks. According to Canada's guide to CEPA 1999, Canada's Domestic Substances List includes substances that were, between January 1, 1984, and December 31, 1986, in commerce in Canada, or were used for commercial manufacturing purposes, or were manufactured in or imported into Canada in a quantity of 100 kilograms or more in any one calendar year. According to Canadian officials, the Domestic Substances List currently contains approximately 23,000 substances from the original list along with an additional 4,470 substances that have been added to the list following assessments of new substances (1994-2014).

[20] According to Canadian officials, it does so by using tools from a broad suite of federal laws, including CEPA 1999, the Canada Consumer Product Safety Act, the Food and Drugs Act, the Pest Control Products Act, and others.

[21] The AICS is the legal device that distinguishes new from existing chemicals. See id. at s 11. According to the NICNAS website, the AICS is a listing of all industrial chemicals in use in Australia between January 1, 1977, and February 28, 1990. In addition, it includes new assessed chemicals and corrections, as well as chemicals that were regulated by other Australian regulators and have since become industrial chemicals. According to NICNAS officials, there are about 38,000 chemicals on the AICS. Industrial chemicals are defined as a chemical element, including a chemical element contained in a mixture; a compound or complex of a chemical element, including such a compound or complex contained in a

mixture; and a naturally-occurring chemical or a substance of unknown or variable composition, complex reaction products or biological materials. The statute notes that this definition does not include an article, as defined by the Act, a radioactive chemical, or a mixture. Industrial Chemicals Notification and Assessment Act 1989, (Cth) S 6 (Austl.).

[22] WHO's IARC Monographs Programme does this through the use of scientific principles and general operating procedures published in a IARC Monographs Preamble document. See World Health Organization, International Agency for Research on Cancer, IARC Monographs on the Evaluation of Carcinogenic Risks to Humans, Preamble (Lyon France: 2006), accessed November 4, 2014, http://monographs.iarc.fr/ENG/Preamble/CurrentPreamble.pdf.

[23] Persistence refers to an attribute of a substance that describes the length of time that the substance remains in a particular environment before it is physically removed or chemically or biologically transformed. Bioaccumulation refers to the progressive increase in the amount of a substance in an organism or part of an organism that occurs because the rate of intake exceeds the organism's ability to remove the substance from the body.

[24] Health Canada, Final Integrated Framework for the Health-Related Components of Categorization of the Domestic Substances List Under CEPA 1999 (Ottawa, Canada: 2009).

[25] Under CEPA 1999, a substance is considered toxic if it is entering or may enter the environment in a quantity or concentration or under conditions that: (a) have or may have an immediate or long-term harmful effect on the environment or its biological diversity; (b) constitute or may constitute a danger to the environment on which life depends; or (c) constitute or may constitute a danger in Canada to human life or health. CEPA 1999 § 64.

[26] Australian Government, Department of Health, National Industrial Chemicals Notification and Assessment Scheme, Inventory Multi-tiered Assessment and Prioritisation (IMAP) Framework (August 2013), accessed April 21, 2014, http://www.nicnas.gov.au/chemical-information/imap-assessments/the-imap-framework.

[27] Program officials developed their initial focus on about 3,000 chemicals based on what is currently known about their effects on human health or the environment.

[28] An IMAP assessment goes to one of three levels of depth: Tier I, Tier II, and Tier III. The data used, assessment approach, and output for each tier reflects the increasing resources needed for the assessment.

[29] Over time, the scope of the program has expanded beyond chemicals to include other potentially cancer-causing agents, such as occupational exposures, lifestyle factors (e.g., smoking), and other potentially carcinogenic exposures. The program reviews agents, which are defined to include specific chemicals, groups of related chemicals, complex mixtures, occupational or environmental exposures, cultural or behavioral practices, biological organisms, and physical agents.

[30] The program also chooses working group members who have no real or apparent conflicts of interests and gives consideration to demographic diversity and balance of scientific findings and views.

[31] For example, WHO International Programme on Chemical Safety, Guidelines for the Preparation of Concise International Chemical Assessment Documents (May 2002), accessed July 31, 2015, http://www.who.int/ipcs/publications/cicad/en/CICAD_Guidelines_sept-2002.pdf.

[32] IPCS produces different types of assessments and, according to an IPCS official, these different types of assessments generally follow similar processes. However, some assessments undergo an additional step following peer review in which a standing program board provides guidance on how to address peer review comments and determines whether

those comments have been appropriately addressed. Other assessments do not undergo review by this standing board.

[33] The Canada Gazette is the official newspaper of the Government of Canada and publishes regularly, among other things, new and proposed regulations, and an assortment of government notices.

[34] Environment Canada, Regulations and Other Instruments, accessed August 6, 2015, http://ec.gc.ca/lcpecepa/eng/regulations/default.cfm?n=9E7794D4-1.

[35] Environment Canada, Pollution Prevention (P2) Plans, accessed June 29, 2015, http://ec.gc.ca/lcpecepa/default.asp?lang=En&n=BC71EA4E-1.

[36] Environment Canada, Administrative Agreements, accessed June 17, 2015, http://www.ec.gc.ca/lcpecepa/default.asp?lang=En&n=9A610C9B-1.

[37] Environment Canada, The Significant New Activity Provisions under CEPA 1999, accessed June 30, 2015, http://www.ec.gc.ca/lcpe-cepa/default.asp?Lang=En&n=9EFCCB36-1.

[38] Environment Canada, Guidelines, Objectives and Codes of Practice, accessed June 29, 2015, http://www.ec.gc.ca/lcpe-cepa/default.asp?lang=En&n=2952CB83-1. The website also notes that guidelines or objectives (but not codes of practice) may also be prepared to indicate government policy direction.

[39] Environment Canada, Environmental Emergency (E2) Plans, accessed June 17, 2015, http://www.ec.gc.ca/lcpecepa/default.asp?lang=En&n=77C8541E-1.

[40] Canadian Environmental Protection Act, 1999, S.C. 1999, c. 3, as amended (Can.) [hereinafter CEPA 1999].

[41] In Canada, such chemicals are on the Domestic Substances List, which, according to Canada's guide to CEPA 1999, includes substances that were, between January 1, 1984, and December 31, 1986, in commerce in Canada, or were used for commercial manufacturing purposes, or were manufactured in or imported into Canada in a quantity of 100 kilograms or more in any one calendar year. A substance as defined under Canadian law includes any distinguishable kind of organic or inorganic matter, whether animate or inanimate, that is capable of being released as a single substance, an effluent, emission, waste, or a mixture into the Canadian environment. In Australia, such chemicals are on the Australian Inventory of Chemical Substances (AICS), which is the legal device that distinguishes new from existing chemicals. See id. at s 11. According to NICNAS documentation, the AICS is a listing of all industrial chemicals in use in Australia between January 1, 1977, and February 28, 1990. In addition, it includes new assessed chemicals and corrections, as well as chemicals that were regulated by other Australian regulators and have since become industrial chemicals. Also according to NICNAS documentation, industrial chemicals include chemicals used in solvents, adhesives, plastics, paints, inks, fuels, or laboratory reagents, as well as in refrigeration, cosmetics, and household cleaning.

[42] By determination, we are referring to each program's bottom-line assessment regarding a chemical's human health effects.

[43] According to Canada's guide to the Canadian Environmental Protection Act, 1999 (CEPA 1999), the Domestic Substances List includes substances that were, between January 1, 1984, and December 31, 1986, in commerce in Canada, or were used for commercial manufacturing purposes, or were manufactured in or imported into Canada in a quantity of 100 kilograms or more in any one calendar year. CEPA 1999 includes any distinguishable kind of organic or inorganic matter, whether animate or inanimate. The list is regularly amended to include additional substances that have been assessed under the act and allowed into Canada. According to Canadian officials, the Domestic Substances List currently contains approximately 23,000 substances from the original list along with an additional

4,470 substances that have been added to the list following assessments of new substances (1994-2014). Environment Canada, A Guide to Understanding the Canadian Environmental Protection Act, 1999 (Dec. 10, 2004), accessed July 27, 2015, http://www.ec.gc.ca/lcpe-cepa/E00B5BD8-13BC-4FBF-9B74- 1013AD5FFC05/Guide04_e.pdf.

[44] Canadian Environmental Protection Act, 1999, S.C. 1999, c. 3, as amended (Can.) [hereinafter CEPA 1999]. In 2006, the Canadian government launched the CMP, which is aimed at reducing the risks posed by chemicals to human health and the environment. For more information on the CMP, see Government of Canada, Overview of the Chemicals Management Plan, accessed February 9, 2015, http://chemicalsubstanceschimiques.gc.ca/alt_formats/pdf/fact-fait/overview-vue-eng.pdf.

[45] According to Canada's guide to CEPA 1999, substances that meet the definition of toxic under CEPA 1999 can be placed on the List of Toxic Substances. A substance's presence on this list alone does not impose specific management measures on the use of the substance. The recommendation for a chemical's addition to this list, however, triggers statutory obligations that require the Canadian government to contemplate and potentially issue risk management measures for that chemical within specified periods.

[46] According to an Environment Canada website, Section 65 of CEPA 1999 mandates the Ministers of the Environment and Health to compile a list to be known as the Virtual Elimination List. The Ministers must specify the level of quantification for each substance on the list and, having done so, must prescribe the quantity or concentration of the substance that may be released into the environment either alone or in combination with any other substance from any source or type of source. The list currently has includes two substances: (1) hexachlorobutadiene, commonly referred to as HCBD, which was added in 2006, and (2) perfluorooctane sulfonate, commonly referred to as PFOS, and its salts, which was added in 2009. Environment Canada, Virtual Elimination List, accessed July 20, 2015, http://www.ec.gc.ca/lcpe-cepa/default.asp?lang=En&n=2F918AD5-1.

[47] Other governments include those within Canada or a member state, or subdivision of a member state, of the Organisation for Economic Co-operation and Development.

[48] Environment Canada, Priority Substances List, accessed July 17, 2015, http://www.ec.gc.ca/lcpecepa/default.asp?lang=En&n=C6C230D5-1.

[49] Persistence refers to an attribute of a substance that describes the length of time that the substance remains in a particular environment before it is physically removed or chemically or biologically transformed. Bioaccumulation refers to the progressive increase in the amount of a substance in an organism or part of an organism that occurs because the rate of intake exceeds the organism's ability to remove the substance from the body.

[50] Environment Canada and Health Canada, Approach for identification of chemicals and polymers as risk assessment priorities under Part 5 of the Canadian Environmental Protection Act, 1999 (CEPA 1999), (2014), accessed December 4, 2014, http://www.ec.gc.ca/ESE-EES/DEFAULT.ASP?LANG=EN&N=A10191AD-1.

[51] The Canada Gazette is the official newspaper of the Government of Canada and publishes, among other things, new and proposed regulations and an assortment of government notices.

[52] According to officials, these mandatory calls for information from industry are authorized under Sections 70 and 71 of CEPA 1999. According to program documentation, Section 70 puts the onus on industries to provide information they possess that reasonably supports the conclusion that a substance is toxic or capable of becoming toxic as defined under CEPA 1999. Section 71 allows the Minister of the Environment to require all parties engaged in an activity involving a substance to provide information for the purpose of assessing whether

the substance is toxic or is capable of becoming toxic, or for the purpose of assessing whether to control, or the manner in which to control, a substance. This includes the authority to request existing information or to require sampling, testing, and the generation of new data.

[53] According to NICNAS documentation, industrial chemicals include chemicals used in solvents, adhesives, plastics, paints, inks, fuels, or laboratory reagents, as well as in refrigeration, cosmetics, and household cleaning. The Industrial Chemicals (Notification and Assessment) Act 1989 defines the term chemical as a chemical element, including a chemical element contained in a mixture; a compound or complex of a chemical element, including such a compound or complex contained in a mixture; or a naturally-occurring chemical or a UVCB substance (a substance of unknown or variable composition, complex reaction products or biological materials). The statute notes that this definition does not include an article, as defined by the Act, a radioactive chemical, or a mixture. See Industrial Chemicals (Notification and Assessment) Act 1989, (Cth) S 6 (Austl.).

[54] The AICS is the legal device that distinguishes new from existing chemicals. See id. at s 11. According to NICNAS documentation, the AICS is a listing of all industrial chemicals in use in Australia between January 1, 1977, and February 28, 1990. In addition, it includes new assessed chemicals and corrections, as well as chemicals that were regulated by other Australian regulators and have since become industrial chemicals.

[55] Australian Government Department of Health, National Industrial Chemicals Notification and Assessment Scheme, Inventory Multi-tiered Assessment and Prioritisation (IMAP) Framework (Aug. 27, 2013), accessed April 21, 2014, http://www.nicnas.gov.au/chemical-information/imap-assessments/the-imap-framework.

[56] Australian Health Ministers' Advisory Council, Scheduling Policy Framework for Medicines and Chemicals, effective date February 1, 2015, accessed June 3, 2015, https://www.tga.gov.au/publication/ahmac-scheduling-policyframework-medicines-and-chemicals.
According to this website, the framework sets out the scheduling process, guidance for amending the Poisons Standard, and the classification system for medicines and chemicals, as well as guidelines for applications, public consultation and confidential information as these relate to scheduling applications. Australian Government Department of Health, Therapeutic Goods Administration, Poisons Standard June 2015, accessed June 25, 2015, https://www.comlaw.gov.au/DETAILS/F2015L00749/DOWNLOAD. The Poisons Standard June 2015 is made under paragraph 52D(2) (b) of Australia's Therapeutic Goods Act 1989.

[57] Safe Work Australia, GHS Hazardous Chemical Information List, accessed July 23, 2015, http://hsis.safeworkaustralia.gov.au/GHSInformation/GHS_Hazardous_Chemical_Information_List.

[58] According to an Environmental Protection Agency (EPA) website, action plans summarize available hazard, exposure, and use information on chemicals; outline the risks that each chemical may present; and identify the specific steps the agency is taking to address those concerns. As of June 2015, EPA has action plans on the following ten chemicals or groups of chemicals: Benzidine Dyes; Bisphenol A (BPA), Hexabromocyclododecane (HBCD); Methylene Diphenyl Diisocyanate (MDI); Nonylphenol and Nonylphenol Ethoxylates; Perfluorinated chemicals (PFC); Penta, octa, and decabromodiphenyl ethers (PBDEs) in products; Phthalates; Short-chain chlorinated paraffins; and Toluene Diisocyanate (TDI). Environmental Protection Agency, Existing Chemicals Action Plans, accessed July 23, 2015, http://www.epa.gov/opptintr/existingchemicals/pubs/ecactionpln.html.

[59] According to the NICNAS website, the NICNAS Bulletin includes non-statutory notices relevant to the administration of NICNAS. The NICNAS Bulletin is published on the first Tuesday of every month and may include information published on the NICNAS website in the month preceding its publication. National Industrial Chemicals Notification and Assessment Scheme, The NICNAS Bulletin, accessed September 15, 2015, http://www.nicnas.gov.au/communications/publications/the-nicnas-bulletin.

[60] World Health Organization, International Agency for Research on Cancer, IARC Monographs on the Evaluation of Carcinogenic Risks to Humans, Preamble (Lyon France, 2006), accessed November 4, 2014, http://monographs.iarc.fr/ENG/Preamble/Current Preamble.pdf.

[61] The other determinations include, "the agent is probably carcinogenic to humans," "the agent is possibly carcinogenic to humans," and, "the agent is not classifiable as to its carcinogenicity to humans."

[62] The Stockholm Convention on Persistent Organic Pollutants, 2256 UNTS 119, is a global treaty to protect human health and the environment from chemicals that remain intact in the environment for long periods, become widely distributed geographically, accumulate in the fatty tissue of humans and wildlife, and have harmful impacts on human health or on the environment. United Nations Environment Programme, Stockholm Convention on Persistent Organic Pollutants, Overview, accessed August, 23, 2015, http://chm.pops.int/TheConvention/Overview/tabid/3351/Default.aspx.

[63] World Health Organization, International Programme on Chemical Safety, Environmental Health Criteria 241, DDT in Indoor Residual Spraying: Human Health Aspects (Geneva Switzerland, 2011), accessed June 25, 2015, http://whqlibdoc.who.int/publi cations/2011/9789241572415_eng.pdf?ua=1.

[64] World Health Organization, WHO Chemical Safety – Activity Report 2014, accessed February 3, 2015, http://www.who.int/ipcs/about_ipcs/activity_report_2014.pdf?ua=1.

[65] Canadian Environmental Protection Act, 1999, S.C. 1999, c. 3, as amended (Can.) [hereinafter CEPA 1999].

[66] Environment Canada, A Guide to Understanding the Canadian Environmental Protection Act, 1999 (Dec. 10, 2004), accessed July 27, 2015, http://www.ec.gc.ca/lcpe-cepa/E00B5BD8-13BC-4FBF-9B74- 1013AD5FFC05/Guide04_e.pdf.

[67] These include instruments under CEPA 1999, as well as other risk management measures that are outside of CEPA 1999, including the regulatory provisions of other governments and voluntary approaches.

[68] For example, Environment Canada, Prohibition of Certain Toxic Substances Regulations, 2012 (SOR/2012-285) (Jan. 2, 2013), accessed August 6, 2015, http://www.ec.gc.ca/lcpe-cepa/eng/regulations/detailReg.cfm?intReg=207 and Environment Canada, Marine Spark-Ignition Engine, Vessel and Off-Road Recreational Vehicle Emission Regulations (SOR/2011-10) (Feb. 16, 2011), accessed August 6, 2015, http://www.ec.gc.ca/lcpe-cepa/eng/regulations/detailReg.cfm?intReg=109.

[69] Environment Canada, Regulations and Other Instruments, accessed August 6, 2015, http://ec.gc.ca/lcpecepa/eng/regulations/default.cfm?n=9E7794D4-1.

[70] Environment Canada, Volatile organic compounds that participate in atmospheric photochemical reactions, accessed July 14, 2015, http://www.ec.gc.ca/toxiques-toxics/Default.asp?lang=En&n=98E80CC6-1&xml=075320D0-CF6E-4261-890E-90725A 29E3C4.

[71] The VOC regulation defines "architectural coating" as "a product to be applied onto or impregnated into a substrate, for use on traffic surfaces such as streets and highways, curbs,

berms, driveways, parking lots, sidewalks and airport runways, or stationary structures, including temporary buildings and their appurtenances, whether installed or detached." Environment Canada, Volatile Organic Compound (VOC) Concentration Limits for Architectural Coatings Regulations (SOR/2009-264) §1 (Sept. 30, 2009), accessed August 6, 2015, http://www.ec.gc.ca/lcpecepa/eng/regulations/detailReg.cfm?intReg=117.

[72] Environment Canada, Frequently Asked Questions – Volatile Organic Compound (VOC) Concentration Limits for Architectural Coatings Regulations, accessed July 17, 2015, http://www.ec.gc.ca/lcpecepa/default.asp?lang=En&n=E335DDC8-1.

[73] Section 6 of CEPA 1999 created the CEPA National Advisory Committee (NAC) for the purpose of enabling national action and avoiding duplication in regulatory activity among governments within Canada. According to the NAC webpage, the role of the Committee can be broadly defined as a platform for advising the Minister(s) of Canada and ensuring a full and open sharing of information between the federal, provincial, territorial, and aboriginal governments on all matters related to the protection of the environment and the management of toxic substances.

[74] Environment Canada, Frequently Asked Questions – Volatile Organic Compound (VOC) Concentration Limits for Architectural Coatings Regulations, accessed July 17, 2015, http://www.ec.gc.ca/lcpecepa/default.asp?lang=En&n=E335DDC8-1.

[75] Environment Canada, Pollution Prevention (P2) Plans, accessed June 29, 2015, http://ec.gc.ca/lcpecepa/default.asp?lang=En&n=BC71EA4E-1.

[76] Ibid.

[77] Environment Canada, Pollution Prevention Planning Notices and Results, accessed September 22, 2015, http://www.ec.gc.ca/planp2-p2plan/default.asp?lang=En&n=BCAA1E50-1.

[78] Environment Canada, Final Report: Pollution Prevention Planning and Acrylonitrile, accessed July 17, 2015, http://www.ec.gc.ca/PLANP2-P2PLAN/58F5925A-30C9-411B-8C24-696BDBCCE60B/ACRYLONITRILE%20FINAL%20REPORT%20JULY%202009.PDF.

[79] Environment Canada, Acrylonitrile, accessed July 20, 2015, https://www.ec.gc.ca/toxiques-toxics/Default.asp?lang=En&n=611706C9-1.

[80] Environment Canada, Final Report: Pollution Prevention Planning and Acrylonitrile, accessed July 17, 2015, http://www.ec.gc.ca/PLANP2-P2PLAN/58F5925A-30C9-411B-8C24-696BDBCCE60B/ACRYLONITRILE%20FINAL%20REPORT%20JULY%202009.PDF.

[81] Environment Canada, A Guide to Understanding the Canadian Environmental Protection Act, 1999 (Dec. 10, 2004), accessed July 27, 2015, http://www.ec.gc.ca/lcpe-cepa/E00B5BD8-13BC-4FBF-9B74-1013AD5FFC05/Guide04_e.pdf and Environment Canada, Administrative Agreements, accessed June 17, 2015, http://www.ec.gc.ca/lcpe-cepa/default.asp?lang=En&n=9A610C9B-1.

[82] Environment Canada, Administrative Agreements, accessed June 17, 2015, http://ec.gc.ca/lcpecepa/default.asp?lang=En&n=9A610C9B-1.

[83] Environment Canada, The Significant New Activity Provisions under CEPA 1999, accessed June 30, 2015, http://www.ec.gc.ca/lcpe-cepa/default.asp?Lang=En&n=9EFCCB36-1.

[84] Officials told us that Significant New Activity provisions are also used to address substances found to be nontoxic as part of the Chemicals Management Plan.

[85] Government of Canada, Significant New Activity (SNAc) Orders and Notices, accessed June 30, 2015, http://chemicalsubstanceschimiques.gc.ca/plan/approach-approche/snac-nac/index-eng.php. 86Ibid.

[87] C.I. Pigment Red 104, or molybdate orange, contains lead compounds including lead chromate and lead molybdate.

[88] The composition of a UVCB could be unknown because the molecular structure or composition is unknown or because it is a complex mixture of different molecules. For example, C.I. Pigment Red 104 is a mixture of lead compounds such as lead chromate and lead molybdate. Other examples of UVCBs include fuel oil, beeswax, and soybean flour.

[89] Canada Gazette. Ottawa, July 18, 2012. SOR/2012-138 to 148 and SI/2012-49 to 54 and 56 to 57. 90Ibid.

[91] Environment Canada, Proposed Risk Management Approach for C.I. Pigment Red 104, accessed July 20, 2015, http://ec.gc.ca/ese-ees/default.asp?lang=En&n=5EC834E2-1.

[92] Canada Gazette. Ottawa, July 18, 2012. SOR/2012-138 to 148 and SI/2012-49 to 54 and 56 to 57.

In: Chemical Risk Assessment Activities … ISBN: 978-1-63485-058-2
Editor: Naomi Sutton

Chapter 3

THE TOXIC SUBSTANCES CONTROL ACT (TSCA): A SUMMARY OF THE ACT AND ITS MAJOR REQUIREMENTS*

Jerry H. Yen

SUMMARY

This report summarizes the Toxic Substances Control Act (TSCA) and the major regulatory programs dealing with chemical production and distribution in U.S. commerce.

President Ford signed TSCA into law on October 11, 1976. Subsequently, five titles were added to address specific concerns—asbestos in 1986 (Title II, P.L. 99-519), radon in 1988 (Title III, P.L. 100-551), lead in 1992 (Title IV, P.L. 102-550), environmental and energy issues in schools in 2007 (Title V, P.L. 110-140), and formaldehyde emissions from composite wood products in 2010 (Title VI, P.L. 111-199). In 2008, Congress added provisions to Title I, Section 6 and Section 12, banning certain activities with respect to elemental mercury (P.L. 110-414).

TSCA authorizes EPA to identify potentially dangerous chemicals in U.S. commerce that should be subject to federal control. The act authorizes EPA to gather and disseminate information about production,

* This is an edited, reformatted and augmented version of a Congressional Research Service publication RL31905, prepared for Members and Committees of Congress dated September 14, 2015.

use, and possible adverse effects to human health and the environment of existing chemicals, and to issue "test rules" that require manufacturers and processors of potentially dangerous chemicals to conduct and report the results of scientific studies to fill information gaps. For chemicals new to U.S. commerce, TSCA requires pre-market screening and regulatory tracking of new chemical products.

If EPA identifies unreasonable risks associated with existing or new chemicals, TSCA requires the agency to initiate rulemaking to reduce risks to a reasonable level. EPA may regulate the manufacture, importation, processing, distribution, use, and/or disposal of chemicals. TSCA provides a variety of regulatory tools to EPA, ranging in severity from a total ban on production, import, and use to a requirement that a product must bear a warning label at the point of sale. However, TSCA directs EPA to use the least burdensome option that can reduce risk to a level that is reasonable, given the benefits provided by the chemical product or process.

Title I of the original statute establishes the core program, directs EPA to control risks from polychlorinated biphenyls (PCBs), and bans certain activities with respect to elemental mercury. Title II directs EPA to set standards for asbestos mitigation in schools and requires asbestos contractors to be trained and certified. Title III directs EPA to provide technical assistance to states that choose to support radon monitoring and control. Title IV provides similar assistance with respect to abatement of lead-based paint hazards. Title V addresses environmental issues at schools, including energy efficiency. Finally, Title VI directs EPA to set standards for emissions of formaldehyde from composite wood products.

In the 114th Congress, there has been debate on legislation that would amend Title I of TSCA (S. 697, S. 725, and H.R. 2576). These bills would revise the chemical evaluation process and the criteria by which chemical substances would be regulated and to address certain other related purposes.

INTRODUCTION

The Environmental Protection Agency (EPA) is responsible for identifying and regulating toxic substances in U.S. commerce under the authority of the Toxic Substances Control Act (TSCA). This report defines key terms, provides a brief history of toxic substances control law, and describes key provisions of TSCA. The report is descriptive rather than analytic, highlights key provisions rather than providing a comprehensive inventory of the act's numerous sections, and addresses authorities and limitations imposed by statute, rather than the status of EPA implementation or other policy issues.

Table 1 lists TSCA as enacted in 1976 and the major amendments to the law. *Table 2* is a table that cross references sections of the *U.S. Code* with corresponding sections of the act.

OVERVIEW

The Toxic Substances Control Act (15 U.S.C. 2601 *et seq.*) authorizes the EPA to screen existing and new chemicals used in manufacturing and commerce to identify potentially dangerous products or uses that should be subject to federal control. Both naturally occurring and synthetic chemicals are subject to TSCA, with the exception of chemicals regulated under other federal laws concerning food, drugs, cosmetics, firearms, ammunition, pesticides, tobacco, or mixtures. EPA may require manufacturers and processors of chemicals to conduct and report the results of tests to determine the effects of potentially dangerous chemicals on living things. Based on test results and other information, EPA must regulate the manufacture, importation, processing, distribution, use, and/or disposal of any chemical that presents an unreasonable risk of injury to human health or the environment. A variety of regulatory tools is available to EPA under TSCA, ranging in severity from a total ban on production, import, and use to a requirement that a product bears a warning label at the point of sale. TSCA directs EPA to use the least burdensome option that can reduce risk to a level that is reasonable, given the benefits provided by the chemical product or process.

Table 1. Toxic Substances Control Act and Major Amendments (codified as 15 U.S.C. 2601-2697)

Year	Act	Public Law Number
1976	Toxic Substances Control Act	P.L. 94-469
1986	Asbestos Hazard Emergency Response Act	P.L. 99-519
1988	Radon Program Development Act	P.L. 100-551
1990	Radon Measurement	P.L.101-508 §10202
1990	Asbestos School Hazard Abatement Reauthorization Act	P.L. 101-637
1992	Residential Lead-Based Paint Hazard Reduction Act of 1992	P.L. 102-550
2007	Energy Independence and Security Act of 2007, subtitle E - Healthy High-Performance Schools	P.L. 110-140
2008	Mercury Export Ban Act of 2008	P.L. 110-414
2010	Formaldehyde Standards for Composite Wood Products Act	P.L. 111-199

The President's Council on Environmental Quality proposed comprehensive federal legislation in 1971 to identify and control potentially dangerous chemicals in U.S. commerce that were not adequately regulated under other environmental statutes. Its report, "Toxic Substances," defined a need for comprehensive legislation to identify and control chemicals whose manufacture, processing, distribution, use, and/or disposal was potentially dangerous and not adequately regulated under other environmental statutes. The House and Senate each passed bills in both the 92nd and 93rd Congresses (in 1972 and 1973, respectively), but controversies over the scope of chemical screening prior to commercial production and distribution, level of costs, and the relationship to other regulatory laws stalled final action. Episodes of environmental contamination—including contamination of the Hudson River and other waterways by PCBs, the threat of stratospheric ozone depletion from chlorofluorocarbon (CFC) emissions, and contamination of agricultural produce by polybrominated biphenyls (PBBs) in the state of Michigan—together with more exact estimates of the costs of imposing toxic substances controls, opened the way for final passage of the legislation. President Ford signed the TSCA into law on October 11, 1976. The original legislation included a single title, which has since been designated Title I.

TSCA (Title I) directs EPA to

- require manufacturers and processors to conduct tests for existing chemicals if (1) their manufacture, distribution, processing, use, or disposal may present an unreasonable risk of injury to health or the environment; or they are to be produced in substantial quantities and the potential for environmental release or human exposure is substantial or significant; (2) existing data are insufficient to predict the effects of human exposure and environmental releases; and (3) testing is necessary to develop such data (§4);
- prevent future risks through pre-manufacture screening and regulatory tracking of new chemical products (§5);
- control unreasonable risks already known, including risks from polychlorinated biphenyls (PCBs), as well as risks for existing chemicals that may be discovered in the future (§6); and
- gather and disseminate information about chemical production, use, and possible adverse effects to human health and the environment (§8).

Authorization for appropriations for these activities and a state grant program for control of toxic substances in the environment expired on September 30, 1983, although appropriations for these programs have continued.

In October 2008, Congress amended TSCA Title I when it enacted the Mercury Export Ban Act of 2008 (P.L. 110-414). It prohibits certain activities with respect to elemental mercury.

Subsequently, five titles have been added to TSCA to address specific concerns—asbestos in 1986 (Title II, P.L. 99-519), radon in 1988 (Title III, P.L. 100-551), lead in 1992 (Title IV, P.L. 102-550), schools in 2007 (Title V, P.L. 110-140), and formaldehyde in 2010 (Title VI, P.L. 111- 199). Title II directs EPA to set standards for asbestos mitigation in schools, and requires asbestos contractors to be trained and certified. Title III directs EPA to provide technical assistance to states that choose to support radon monitoring and control. Title IV provides similar assistance with respect to abatement of lead-based paint hazards. Title V addresses environmental issues at schools, including energy efficiency. Finally, Title VI establishes limits on emissions of formaldehyde from composite wood products.

TITLE I

Testing of Chemicals

Many chemicals, even some in widespread use, are not well characterized in terms of their potential health and environmental effects. One of the major goals of TSCA was to induce the development of test data by producers (i.e., manufacturers, importers, and processors) of chemicals in commerce. Section 4 of TSCA directs EPA to require the development of test data on existing chemicals when certain conditions prevail: (1) the manufacture, processing, distribution, use, or disposal of the chemical "may present an unreasonable risk;" or (2) the chemical is produced in very large volume and there is a potential for a substantial quantity to be released into the environment or for substantial or significant human exposure. Under either condition, EPA must issue a rule requiring tests if (a) existing data are insufficient to resolve the question of safety, and (b) testing is necessary to develop the data.

Because there were more than 55,000 chemicals in U.S. commerce at the time EPA was to begin developing test rules, Congress established a special interagency committee to help EPA determine which chemicals should be considered first, and to coordinate testing needs and efforts among government agencies. At least every six months the Interagency Testing Committee (ITC) must consider candidate chemicals for inclusion on a list of substances that the ITC recommends to EPA for development and promulgation of test rules. TSCA directs the ITC to "designate" a subset of chemicals on the list for EPA action within 12 months. The list can contain no more than 50 "designated" chemicals at any time. When a chemical is designated, EPA has one year to respond by issuing a proposed test rule or a notice explaining why no testing is needed.

TSCA requires the ITC to consider the following factors when it makes listing decisions: (1) quantity of the substance to be manufactured, (2) quantity of the chemical in environmental releases, (3) number of people who will be exposed occupationally and the duration of exposure, (4) extent of non-occupational human exposure, (5) similarity of the chemical to any other chemical known to present an unreasonable risk, (6) existence of data concerning environmental or health effects of the chemical, (7) the quantity of information to be gained by testing, and (8) the availability of facilities and personnel for performing testing. Chemicals known or suspected to cause or contribute to cancer, gene mutations, or birth defects are to be assigned a higher priority. In response to information that indicates "there may be a reasonable basis to conclude that a chemical ... presents or will present a significant risk of serious or widespread harm to human beings from cancer, gene mutations, or birth defects," TSCA requires EPA action to prevent or reduce that risk or publication of a finding that the risk is not unreasonable.

Pre-Manufacture Notification for New Chemicals or Uses

TSCA (§5) requires manufacturers, importers, and processors to notify EPA at least 90 days prior to producing or otherwise introducing a new chemical product into the United States. Any information or test data that is known to, reasonably ascertainable by, or in possession of the notifier, and that might be useful to EPA in evaluating the chemical's potential adverse effects on human health or the environment, must be submitted to EPA at the same time. TSCA also requires EPA to be notified when there are plans to produce, process, or use an existing chemical in a way that differs from previously permitted uses, if the Administrator has determined by rule that new uses of the chemical may produce significant changes in human and environmental exposures and therefore require notification. The 90-day notice provides EPA with the opportunity to evaluate the chemical use and, if necessary, to prohibit or limit such activity before it occurs to prevent unreasonable risk of injury to human health or the environment.

EPA has 45 days after notification (or up to 90 days if it extends the period for good cause) to evaluate the potential risk posed by the chemical. If EPA determines that there is a reasonable basis to conclude that the substance presents or will present an unreasonable risk, the Administrator must promulgate requirements to protect adequately against such risk. Alternatively, EPA may determine that the proposed activity related to a chemical does not present an unreasonable risk; this decision may be based on the available data, or, when no data exist to document the effects of exposure, on what is known about the effects of chemicals in commerce with similar chemical structures and used in similar ways.

The purpose of EPA's screening procedure is to identify potential hazards, and control them before use of a chemical becomes widespread. If data are inadequate to make an informed judgment and (1) manufacture, processing, distribution in commerce, use, or disposal may present an unreasonable risk; or (2) a chemical is to be produced in substantial quantities, and the potential for environmental release or human exposure is substantial or significant, EPA may issue a proposed order to prohibit or limit such activities until sufficient data are submitted.

Although the legislative history of TSCA includes a presumption that testing of new products would take place before they were widely used, either as the chemical was developed, or as its markets grew, TSCA also forbids promulgation of blanket testing requirements for all new chemicals. This reflects concern that uniform testing requirements might stifle innovation in the chemical industry. Thus, EPA must decide which chemicals, or which categories of chemicals, warrant the costs of pre-market testing. EPA reviews approximately 1,000 new chemical manufacturing notices annually.

Regulatory Controls for Hazardous Chemicals

TSCA requires EPA to regulate manufacturing, processing, distribution in commerce, use, or disposal of a chemical if it will present an unreasonable risk of injury to health or the environment, and the risk cannot be reduced to a sufficient degree under another federal law administered by EPA. The alternative means available to EPA for controlling chemical hazards that present unreasonable risks are specified in Section 6 of TSCA. EPA has the authority to

- prohibit or limit the amount of production or distribution of a substance in commerce;
- prohibit or limit the production or distribution of a substance for a particular use;
- limit the volume or concentration of the chemical produced;
- prohibit or regulate the manner or method of commercial use;
- require warning labels and/or instructions on containers or products;
- require notification of the risk of injury to distributors and, to the extent possible, consumers;
- require record-keeping by producers;
- specify disposal methods; and
- require replacement or repurchase of products already distributed.

EPA also may impose any of these requirements in combination or for a specific geographical region. However, EPA is required by TSCA to regulate only "to the extent necessary to protect adequately" against a risk, and to use the "least burdensome" regulatory approach, even in controlling unreasonable risks.

Two chemical substances are directly addressed in Title I: PCBs and elemental mercury. TSCA directs EPA to regulate PCBs and to ban most uses. In addition, TSCA prohibits the sale, distribution, or transfer of elemental mercury by federal agencies.

Information Gathering

Section 8 of TSCA requires EPA to develop and maintain an inventory of all chemicals, or categories of chemicals, manufactured or processed in the United States. The first version of this inventory identified approximately 55,000 chemicals in commerce in 1979. All chemicals not on the inventory are, by definition, "new" and subject to the notification provisions of Section 5. These chemicals must be added to the inventory if they enter U.S. commerce. Chemicals need not be listed if they are only produced in very small quantities for purposes of experimentation or research.

To aid EPA in its duties under TSCA, the agency was granted considerable authority to collect information from industries. EPA may require maintenance of records and reporting of chemical identities, names, and molecular structures; categories of use; amounts manufactured and processed for each category of use; descriptions of byproducts resulting from manufacture, processing, use, and disposal; environmental and health effects; number of individuals exposed; number of employees exposed and the duration of exposure; and manner or method of chemical disposal.

Manufacturers, processors, and distributors of chemicals are required to maintain records of significant adverse reactions to health or the environment alleged to have been caused by a substance or mixture. Records of adverse effects on the health of employees must be retained for 30 years from the date of reporting. Industry also must submit lists and copies of health and safety studies. Studies showing adverse effects previously unknown must be submitted to EPA as soon as they are completed or discovered.

Imminent Hazards

Section 7 provides EPA authority to take emergency action through the district courts to control a chemical substance or mixture which presents an imminent and unreasonable risk of serious widespread injury to health or the environment.

Relation to Other Laws

Section 9 requires EPA to report cases of chemical risk to other federal agencies with the authority to prevent or reduce the risk. If the other agency determines that the activity does not present the risk described by EPA in its report, or initiates action under the law to protect against the risk, TSCA prohibits EPA from taking regulatory action with respect to such risk. For statutes under EPA's jurisdiction, TSCA gives the Administrator discretion to decide if a risk can best be handled under the authority of TSCA.

Enforcement and Judicial Review

Section 11 authorizes EPA to inspect any facilities subject to TSCA requirements and to issue subpoenas requiring attendance and testimony of witnesses, production of reports and documents, answers to questions and other necessary information. Section 13 mandates TSCA enforcement at the national borders by the Department of the Treasury.

Section 15 identifies acts prohibited under TSCA, while Section 16 describes penalties for acts violating these prohibitions, as well as recourse available to anyone accused of such violations. Section 16 authorizes civil penalties, not to exceed $25,000 per violation per day, and affords the defendant an opportunity to request a hearing before an order is issued and to petition for judicial review of an order after it is issued. Criminal penalties also are authorized for willful violations. Section 17 provides jurisdiction to U.S. district courts in civil actions to enforce TSCA Section 15 by restraining or compelling actions that violate or comply with it, respectively. Chemicals may be seized and condemned if their manufacture, processing, or distribution violated the act.

Section 19 authorizes any person to file a petition for judicial review of specified rules within 60 days of issuance under TSCA. The court is directed to set aside specified rules if they are not supported by substantial evidence in the rulemaking record taken as a whole.

Section 20 authorizes civil suits by any person against any person in violation of the act. It also authorizes suits against EPA to compel performance of nondiscretionary actions under TSCA. Section 21 provides the public with the right to petition for the issuance, amendment, or repeal of a rule requiring toxicity testing of a chemical, regulation of the chemical, or reporting.

Confidential Business Information

Section 14 provides broad protection of proprietary confidential information about chemicals in commerce. Disclosure by EPA employees of such information generally is not permitted, except to other federal employees, or when necessary to protect health or the environment. Data from health and safety studies of chemicals are not protected unless their disclosure would reveal a chemical process or chemical proportion in a mixture. Wrongful disclosure of confidential data by federal employees is prohibited, and may result in criminal penalties.

Chemical Categories

Section 26 allows EPA to impose regulatory controls on categories of chemicals, rather than on a case-by-case basis. However, EPA cannot regulate a group merely because it is composed of new chemical substances.

State Preemption

TSCA Section 18 preempts state actions that establish or continue in effect requirements applicable to a chemical substance or mixture that is regulated under TSCA Section 5 or 6, unless the state requirement is identical to the federal requirement, implements another federal law, or prohibits use of the substance or mixture within the state. However, a state may ask EPA to allow a state requirement that provides a significantly higher degree of protection from risk than does the federal requirement.

Other Provisions

TSCA Section 10 directs EPA to conduct and coordinate among federal agencies research, development, and monitoring that is necessary to the purposes of the act.

Section 12 excludes chemical products manufactured for export from TSCA requirements except for reporting and record keeping requirements in Section 8. In 2008, Congress excluded elemental mercury from this exemption, banning its export beginning in 2013, with the exception of mercury contained in coal. Other exemptions for essential uses may be granted by rule.

Section 22 waives compliance when in the interest of national defense.

Section 23 provides protection of employees who assist in carrying out the provisions of the act (i.e., “whistle-blowers”).

The potential effects of TSCA rules on employment must be monitored by EPA, according to Section 24.

Section 25 mandates study of the need for indemnification of people affected by federal laws administered by EPA and of the feasibility of establishing a standard classification system for chemical substances and of storing and retrieving information about them.

Section 26 authorizes data sharing and cooperative action to facilitate TSCA implementation between EPA and other federal agencies. It also authorizes collection of fees for EPA processing of data submitted in response to an order under Section 4 or 5. EPA is directed to establish an office to assist the regulated community. The agency also must establish a procedure to ensure disclosure of financial interests in the regulated community by EPA employees. Final orders issued under TSCA must contain a statement of basis and purpose. Finally, Section 26 established within EPA a new Assistant Administrator for Toxic Substances.

TSCA Section 27 authorizes research and development of test methods for chemicals by the Public Health Service in cooperation with EPA.

Grants to states are authorized by Section 28 to establish and operate programs to prevent or eliminate unreasonable risks to health or the environment.

Section 29 authorized appropriations through 1983. An annual report is mandated by Section 30.

TITLE II. (ASBESTOS IN BUILDINGS)

Growing public concern about the presence of potentially hazardous asbestos in buildings, especially in schools, led to congressional efforts to address this problem. Title II of TSCA, the Asbestos Hazard Emergency Response Act (AHERA), was enacted in 1986 (P.L. 99-519) and amended in July 1988 (P.L. 100-368). It required EPA to set standards by October 1987, for responding to the presence of asbestos in schools. The standards, set at levels adequate to protect public health and the environment, identify appropriate response actions that depend on the physical condition of asbestos. Schools, in turn, were required to inspect for asbestos-containing material, and to develop and implement a plan for managing any such material. Plans for managing asbestos were to be submitted by schools before May 1989, and implementation was to begin by July 1989. The law contains no deadlines for schools to complete implementation.

Title II requires asbestos contractors and analytical laboratories to be certified, and schools to use certified persons for abatement work. Training and accreditation requirements also apply to inspectors, contractors, and workers performing asbestos abatement work in all public and commercial buildings. EPA may award training grants to nonprofit organizations for asbestos health and safety programs. However, authorization of appropriations for this grant program expired September 30, 1995. Other Title II requirements (such as mandates that buildings be inspected for asbestos) have not been extended to non-school buildings.

To enforce requirements, TSCA authorizes EPA to take emergency action with respect to schools if school officials do not act to protect children. The act also authorizes citizen action with respect to asbestos-containing material in a school and to compel action by EPA, either through administrative petition or judicial action. Civil penalties not to exceed $5,000 are authorized for violations such as failing to conduct an inspection or to develop a school management plan.

Concern about how schools would pay for required actions was addressed in separate legislation (the Asbestos School Hazard Abatement Act of 1984, or ASHAA, P.L. 98-377). It established a program offering grants and interest-free loans to schools with serious asbestos problems and demonstrated financial need. Although EPA for several years did not request funding for this program, Congress appropriated funds. Authorization of appropriations for this program expired September 30, 1995, and Congress has not appropriated funds since FY1993; a total of $382 million in grant and loan funds were appropriated from FY1984 through FY1993. Repaid ASHAA loans are returned to an Asbestos Trust Fund, established in TSCA Title II, to become a dedicated source of revenues for future asbestos control projects.

TITLE III. (RADON PROGRAMS)

In October 1988, Congress amended TSCA by adding Title III—Indoor Radon Abatement (15 U.S.C. 2661 *et seq.,* P.L. 100-551). The basic purpose of Title III is to provide financial and technical assistance to the states that choose to support radon monitoring and control; neither monitoring nor abatement of radon is required by the act.

Title III required EPA to update its pamphlet "A Citizen's Guide to Radon," to develop model construction standards and techniques for controlling radon levels within new buildings, and to provide technical assistance to states. EPA is to provide technical assistance by establishing an information clearinghouse; publishing public information materials;

establishing a national database of radon levels detected, organized by state; providing information to professional organizations representing private firms involved in building design and construction; submitting to Congress a plan for providing financial and technical assistance to states; operating cooperative projects with states; conducting research to develop, test, and evaluate radon measurement methods and protocols; developing and demonstrating new methods of radon measurement and mitigation, including methods that are suitable for use in nonresidential child care facilities; operating a voluntary program to rate radon measurement and mitigation devices and methods and the effectiveness of private firms and individuals offering radon-related services; and designing and implementing training seminars. The proficiency rating program and certification for training programs collect fees for service, and therefore are meant to be self-supporting, but Congress authorized $1.5 million to be appropriated to establish these programs. Congress authorized $3 million to be appropriated for each of three years beginning in 1989 for the other provisions of Sections 303, 304, and 305.

A matching grant program was established for the purpose of assisting states in developing and implementing programs for radon assessment and mitigation. For this program, $30 million was authorized to be appropriated over three years, with funds targeted to states or projects that made efforts to ensure adoption of EPA's model construction standards and techniques for new buildings; gave preference to low-income persons; or addressed serious and extensive radon contamination problems or had the potential to reduce risk or to develop innovative assessment techniques, mitigation measures, or management approaches.

Other sections of Title III require EPA to conduct a study to determine the extent of radon contamination in schools; identify and list areas of the United States with a high probability of having high levels of indoor radon; make grants or cooperative agreements to establish and operate at least three regional radon training centers; and provide guidance to federal agencies on radon measurement, risk assessment, and remedial measures.

All authorizations for appropriations specific to this title expired September 30, 1991, although appropriations have continued.

TITLE IV. (LEAD EXPOSURE REDUCTION)

The 102nd Congress added Title IV to TSCA when it enacted the Residential Lead-Based Paint Hazard Reduction Act of 1992 as Title X in the

Housing and Community Development Act of 1992 (P.L. 102-550). TSCA Title IV aims to accelerate federal efforts to reduce risks to young children who daily are exposed to lead-based paint in their homes. In addition, it was intended to stimulate development of lead inspection and hazard abatement services in the private sector, while ensuring that the services provided and any products employed are reliable and effective in reducing risk. To these ends, Title IV directs EPA to

- promulgate definitions of lead-contaminated dust, lead-contaminated soil, and lead-based paint hazards;
- ensure that people engaged in detection and control of lead hazards are properly trained and that contractors are certified;
- publish requirements for the accreditation of training programs for workers;
- develop criteria to evaluate the effectiveness of commercial products used to detect or reduce risks associated with lead-based paint;
- establish protocols, criteria, and minimum performance standards for laboratory analysis of lead in paint films, soil, and dust;
- establish a program to certify laboratories as qualified to test substances for lead content; and
- publish and distribute to the public a list of certified or accredited environmental sampling laboratories.

Title IV explicitly applies these requirements to federal facilities and activities that may create a lead hazard.

In addition, Congress directed EPA to conduct a study of lead hazards due to renovation and remodeling activities that may incidentally disturb lead-based paint. EPA is required to promulgate guidelines for the renovation and remodeling of buildings or other structures when these activities might create a hazard.

Title IV directs EPA to establish a clearinghouse and hotline to distribute information about the hazards of lead-based paint, how to avoid exposure and reduce risk, and new technologies for removing or immobilizing lead-based paint. In addition, Congress mandated development of a lead hazard information pamphlet; public education and outreach activities for health professionals, the general public, homeowners, landlords, tenants, consumers of home improvement products, the residential real estate industry, and the home renovation industry; and information to be distributed by retailers of home improvement products to provide consumers with practical information related to the hazards of renovation where lead-based paint may be present.

Title IV authorizes states to propose programs to train and certify inspectors and contractors engaged in the detection or control of lead-based paint hazards. States also may develop the required informational pamphlets. TSCA requires EPA to promulgate a model state program that may be adopted by any state. Congress gave EPA the authority to approve or disapprove authorization for state proposals and to provide grants for states to develop and implement authorized programs. A federal program must be established, administered, and enforced by EPA in each state without an authorized program.

The Department of Health and Human Services also has responsibilities under Title IV of TSCA. It mandates a study by the Centers for Disease Prevention and Control (CDC) and the National Institute for Environmental Health Sciences to determine the sources of lead exposure to children who have elevated lead levels in their bodies. The National Institute for Occupational Safety and Health is directed to study ways of reducing occupational exposure to lead during abatement activities.

The act established a rule-making docket to ensure the availability to the general public of all documents submitted to agencies that are relevant to regulatory decisions pursuant to this legislation. The docket is required to include the drafts of all proposed rules submitted by EPA to the President's Office of Management and Budget (OMB), written comments on the drafts, and written responses to comments. In addition, the agency must provide an explanation for any major change to a proposed rule that appears in the final rule, and such changes may not be made based on information not filed in the docket. Dockets are required to be established in each EPA regional office.

Congress authorized to be appropriated "such sums as may be necessary" for TSCA Title IV.

In addition to amending TSCA, Title X of the Housing and Community Development Act of 1992 authorized grants to states for risk assessments and lead-based paint removal and immobilization in private housing for low-income residents; establishing state training, certification, or accreditation programs for inspectors and abatement contractors; and research at the Department of Housing and Urban Development (HUD). Authorization for appropriations for these grants expired September 30, 1994, but appropriations have continued. Title X directed HUD to establish guidelines for federally supported work involving risk assessments, inspections, interim controls, and abatement of lead-based paint hazards. In addition, the National Institute for

Occupational Safety and Health (NIOSH) was provided $10 million for training people who remove or immobilize paint.

TITLE V. (REDUCING RISKS IN SCHOOLS)

At the end of 2007, the 110th Congress added a fifth title to TSCA, subtitled Healthy High-Performance Schools. Enacted as Title IV, Subtitle E (§461) of P.L. 110-140, the Energy Independence and Security Act of 2007, TSCA Title V authorizes EPA to establish a state grant program to provide technical assistance for EPA programs to schools and develop and implement state school environmental health programs. State programs must include standards for school building design, construction, and renovation, and identify ongoing school building environmental problems and recommended solutions. Environmental problems specifically mentioned in the law include "contaminants, hazardous substances, and pollutant emissions." EPA's authority to provide grants expires five years after the date of enactment.

Title V requires the EPA Administrator, in consultation with the Secretary of Education and the Secretary of Health and Human Services, to issue voluntary guidelines within 18 months of Title V enactment for selecting sites for schools (presumably new schools). The guidelines are to account for the "special vulnerability of children to hazardous substances or pollution exposures in any case in which the potential for contamination at a potential school site exists," modes of transportation available to students and staff, efficient use of energy, and potential use of a school at the site as an emergency shelter.

Title V also requires the EPA Administrator, in consultation with the Secretary of Education and the Secretary of Health and Human Services, to issue voluntary guidelines within two years of enactment for developing and implementing state environmental health programs for schools. These guidelines must take into account the findings of federal initiatives established under "relevant federal law with respect to school facilities," including initiatives related to water and energy conservation authorized by Sections 431 through 441, and work related to high-performance green buildings authorized by Section 492 of P.L. 110-140. In particular, the guidelines must take into account "environmental problems, contaminants, hazardous substances, and pollutant emissions"; natural day lighting; ventilation; heating and cooling; moisture control and mold; maintenance, cleaning, and pest control; acoustics; and "other issues relating to the health, comfort, productivity, and performance of occupants of the school facilities." In addition, Title V requires that the guidelines provide "technical assistance on siting, design, management, and operation of school facilities"; collaborate with children's environmental health centers in school environmental investigations"; assist states and the public to better understand and improve the environmental health of children; and take into account "the special vulnerability of children in low-income and minority communities to exposures from contaminants, hazardous substances, and pollutant emissions."

Several provisions in Title V refer to entities established under other sections of the Energy Independence and Security Act of 2007 (P.L. 110-140). For example, Title V contains directives for the Federal Director of the Office of Federal High-Performance Green Buildings in the General Services Administration, which was created by Section 436(a). In addition, there is reference to the national high-performance green building clearinghouse established in Section 423(1) "to carry out public outreach to inform individuals and entities of the information and services [related to high-performance green buildings] available governmentwide." Title V requires the Federal Director to ensure, "to the maximum extent practicable," that the public clearinghouse "receives and makes available information on the exposure of children to environmental hazards in school facilities." The EPA Administrator is directed to prepare an annual report to Congress on activities carried out under Title V authority, and this report also must be made available to the public through the clearinghouse.

For the purposes of carrying out the provisions of Title V, Congress authorized appropriations of $1.5 million annually through 2013.

TITLE VI. (LIMITING FORMALDEHYDE EMISSIONS)

In July 2010, Congress enacted the Formaldehyde Standards for Composite Wood Products Act (P.L. 111-199), adding a new Title VI to TSCA. The new title mandates specific formaldehyde emission standards for hardwood plywood, medium-density fiberboard, and particleboard that is sold, supplied, offered for sale, or manufactured in the United States. The standards are phased in over two years from enactment and are based on the voluntary national formaldehyde emissions standards established by ASTM International (formerly known as the American Society for Testing and Materials), method ASTM E-1333-96 (2002).

The standards apply to plywood, particleboard, and medium-density fiberboard in the form of an unfinished panel or incorporated into a finished good. Certain products are excluded, including many forms of lumber and panels used for outdoor applications, such as structural plywood, prefabricated wood I-joists, most windows, antiques or other previously owned goods, and composite wood products used inside automobiles, trucks, rail cars, boats, and aircraft.

EPA is required to promulgate regulations ensuring compliance with the emission standards and must include provisions relating to labeling, chain of custody requirements, sell-through provisions; ultra-low-emitting formaldehyde resins, finished goods, third-party testing and certification; auditing and reporting of third-party certifiers; recordkeeping; enforcement, laminated products; and exceptions for products and components containing "de minimis amounts" of composite wood products. The new law prohibits stockpiling of products manufactured before the effective date of the act for sale after that date. Also prohibited is any requirement for labeling products manufactured prior to the "designated date of manufacture."

P.L. 111-199 requires an annual report to Congress on the status of implementation and the extent to which relevant industries have achieved compliance. Finally, the act directs the Secretary of Housing and Urban Development to update regulations concerning formaldehyde emissions from composite wood in manufactured homes (24 Code of Federal Regulations 3280.308) to ensure that the standards established by TSCA Title VI are implemented.

Table 2. Major *U.S. Code* Sections, Toxic Substances Control Act (codified as 15 U.S.C. 2601-2692)

15 U.S.C.	Section Title	Toxic Substances Control Act (as amended)
Subchapter I	Control of Toxic Substances	
2601	Findings, policy and intent	§2
2602	Definitions	§3
2603	Testing of chemical substances and mixtures	§4
2604	Manufacturing and processing notices	§5
2605	Regulation of hazardous chemical substances and mixtures	§6
2606	Imminent hazards	§7
2607	Reporting and retention of information	§8

Table 2. (Continued)

15 U.S.C.	Section Title	Toxic Substances Control Act (as amended)
2608	Relationship to other federal laws	§9
2609	Research, development, collection, dissemination, and utilization of data	§10
2610	Inspections and subpoenas	§11
2611	Exports	§12
2612	Entry into customs territory of the United States	§13
2613	Disclosure of data	§14
2614	Prohibited acts	§15
2615	Penalties	§16
2616	Specific enforcement and seizure	§17
2617	Preemption	§18
2618	Judicial review	§19
2619	Citizens' civil actions	§20
2620	Citizens' petitions	§21
2621	National defense waiver	§22
2622	Employee protection	§23
2623	Employment effects	§24
2624	Studies	§25
2625	Administration	§26
2626	Development and evaluation of test methods	§27
2627	State programs	§28
2628	Authorization of appropriations	§29
2629	Annual report	§30
Subchapter II	Asbestos Hazard Emergency Response	
2641	Congressional findings and purpose	§201
2642	Definitions	§202
2643	EPA regulations	§203
2644	Requirements if EPA fails to promulgate regulations	§204
2645	Submission to state Governor	§205
2646	Contractor and laboratory accreditation	§206
2647	Enforcement	§207
2648	Emergency authority	§208
2649	State and federal law	§209
2650	Asbestos contractors and local educational agencies	§210
2651	Public protection	§211
2652	Asbestos ombudsman	§212
2653	EPA study of asbestos-containing material in public buildings	§213
2654	Transition rules	§214
2655	Worker protection	§215

15 U.S.C.	Section Title	Toxic Substances Control Act (as amended)
2656	Training grants	§216
Subchapter III	Indoor Radon Abatement	
2661	National goal	§301
2662	Definitions	§302
2663	EPA's citizen guide	§303
2664	Model construction standards and techniques	§304
2665	Technical assistance to states for radon programs	§305
2666	Grant assistance to states for radon programs	§306
2667	Radon in schools	§307
2668	Regional radon training centers	§308
2669	Study of radon in federal buildings	§309
2670	Regulations	§310
2671	Additional authorizations	§311
Subchapter IV	Lead Exposure Reduction	
2681	Definitions	§401
2682	Lead-based paint activities training and certification	§402
2683	Identification of dangerous levels of lead	§403
2684	Authorized state programs	§404
2685	Lead abatement and measurement	§405
2686	Lead hazard information pamphlet	§406
2687	Regulations	§407
2688	Control of lead-based paint at federal facilities	§408
2689	Prohibited acts	§409
2690	Relationship to other federal law	§410
2691	General provisions relating to administrative proceedings	§411
2692	Authorization of appropriations	§412
Subchapter V	Healthy High-Performance Schools	
2695	Grants for healthy school environments	§501
2695a	Model guidelines for siting of school facilities	§502
2695b	Public outreach	§503
2695c	Environmental health program	§504
2695d	Authorization of appropriations	§505
Subchapter VI	Formaldehyde Standards for Composite Wood Products	
2697	Formaldehyde Standards	§601

Note: This table shows only the major code sections. For more detail and to determine when a section was added, the reader should consult the official printed version of the U.S. Code.

INDEX

A

B

C

D

E

F

G

H

I

P

Q

R

S

T

U

V

W

Z